"I can't think of a more timely book, or a more timely topic. As authors Cassandra Dahnke and Tomás Spath point out, "We the people of this United States of America have become a nation divided against ourselves." And we see the effects of these divisions in every area of our common life, not just in our political life. We are impatient behind the wheel, we speak rudely to each other, we don't listen attentively even to members of our families. And our relationships with each other in the political arena are even more fractured. In this carefully constructed yet easy to absorb book, the authors outline 10 simple, practical steps to help bring us into relationship with each other once again. I urge you to buy and read this book – and watch your life change."

- Sandy Wilder, Host, "Austin Faith Dialogue" TV show

RECLAIMING CIVILITY IN THE PUBLIC SQUARE

10 RULES THAT WORK

CASSANDRA DAHNKE
AND
TOMÁS SPATH
WITH
DONNA BOWLING

"From Civility comes Hope.
From Hope comes Transformation.
From Transformation comes Engagement.
From Engagement comes Strength."
- Cassandra Dahnke

WingSpan Press

Printed in the United States of America

Published by WingSpan Press, Livermore, CA
www.wingspanpress.com

The WingSpan name, logo and colophon are the trademarks of WingSpan Publishing.

ISBN 978-1-59594-150-3

First edition 2007

Library of Congress Control Number 2007924881

To our families,
with love and gratitude for their
encouragement, support and prayers.

TABLE OF CONTENTS

PREFACE

"Enlighten the people generally, and tyranny and oppression of body and mind will vanish like evil spirits at the dawn of day."
- Thomas Jefferson

In the new millennium, after almost 30 years of law practice, I enrolled at Austin Presbyterian Theological Seminary to study the wisdom of countless generations as expressed in the teachings of my Christian faith. I sought a better foundation from which to address the ethical issues that had become my focus. Beyond the expected benefits of a seminary education, I found myself blessed in countless unexpected ways. One of those blessings was meeting Rev. Cassandra Dahnke, my next-door neighbor in the dorm. We were older commuting students who left our families to live in Austin on week days while attending classes, and we found we had many things in common.

As Cassandra and I became better acquainted, she told me about the Institute for Civility in Government (referred to in this book as "the Institute") during our regular walks around the campus of the University of Texas. Cassandra and her colleague, Tomás Spath, had founded the Institute as an outgrowth of their experiences on trips to Washington, D.C. on behalf of the Presbyterian Church. During those trips they escorted members of the church to briefings and meetings with their Congressional representatives. Cassandra also described the Institute's process for modeling civility through engaging young people in dialogue with their elected representatives. I urged Cassandra during our walks and following graduation to share the story of the Institute with a wider audience. She wisely pointed out that their work with the Institute, plus their responsibilities as pastors of churches, left her and Tomás with little time for writing.

Eventually I did something everyone knows is dangerous--I volunteered. What follows is the story of the Institute for Civility in

Government woven together from stories provided by Cassandra and Tomás and others involved with the Institute. In addition to these stories, the book includes the rules for nurturing civility that Cassandra and Tomás have developed while working with the Institute. Cassandra and Tomás, as well as the others they have inspired through the Institute, are convinced that we can reclaim civility in the public square.

We believe their story will convince you as well. The concepts presented are worthy of practice, not just through participation in the common civic life of our representative democracy, but also in the other spheres of our lives in community. Civility is needed not only in our political process, but also in the business world, the church, the family, and anywhere else we humans come together.

For those at all familiar with this country's civic life, writing a book titled RECLAIMING CIVILITY IN THE PUBLIC SQUARE may sound like a naïve endeavor. Seminary teaches a realistic view of human nature with its capacity for both good and evil. We are well aware there are people who will want no part in encouraging civility. They will claim their right to be as uncivil as they please. This book offers no magic formula for changing these difficult people. We believe, however, that those people are a minority.

Before you decide civility is an impossible dream, we challenge you to read the stories of those who have been involved in the work of the Institute. Their experiences demonstrate that the rules described in this book work in the imperfect world where we encounter each other politically. These rules are grounded in the human desire and capacity for living in community. We offer concrete evidence that civility is not only necessary to our common life, but also readily available to us if we will simply accept the challenge and put these rules into practice.

The book describes what those working with the Institute have learned about civility. It tells how to practice and model civility in diverse groups while grappling with the tough issues we face in our common life. Civility is discussed through the presentation and illustration of specific rules related to such concepts as listening, respect, relationship and trust. Stories demonstrate how the rules work in practice within the sphere of public life.

Practicing what the founders and members of the Institute have learned will contribute to an increase in civility in our society at all levels. We also believe learning how to effectively participate in the public square by following these rules will encourage increased participation in our democratic processes--participation that is essential if our democracy is to survive and have a vibrant future. Whether we are aware of it or not, all of us are involved in politics regularly--for politics is merely another name for the way we carry out our human relationships in our larger communities.

The nature of our relationships is determined by the actions and attitudes of each individual who participates in those relationships. If we want the nature of our political environment to be more civil in this country, we must start at the basic level of our one-on-one human interactions. This book describes how to engage in dialogue with greater civility and thus more effectively as we come together in the public square to address the common problems we face.

My thanks to Esther Crosby, Quart Graves, Mary Holcomb, Kathy Nobles, Rebecca Reyna, and Chuck Seidel for graciously sharing their experiences with the Church in Washington and the Institute. They have related the very personal ways those experiences have changed their perceptions and actions as they have learned to participate more fully and effectively in civic life. Thanks also to Linda Rae, Mayor Ken Corley and Michael Robinson for allowing us to share their stories. Special thanks to the Temple Story Tellers for reading and gently suggesting improvements to the drafts of this book. I am especially grateful to Chris Boldt for volunteering her talents as editor and for her faithful assistance in reviewing and improving many drafts. Thank you, John Bowling, for your unflagging support of this project and your encouragement of my writing as well as for reading and listening to me read the manuscript.

Finally, I owe an immense debt of gratitude to Cassandra and Tomás for their patience with my efforts to faithfully tell their story. Through the writing of this book I have been privileged to come to know them better. I am blessed beyond measure by their friendship. May you be as blessed in the reading as I have been in the telling, and may you accept the challenge to put these simple rules into practice for the betterment of our common life in the public square.

Donna Curtis Bowling, J.D., M.A.T.S.

For seven years we led legislative conferences in Washington, D.C. Called "The Church in Washington," these conferences helped average citizens connect with the government in personal and fulfilling ways. In the process, we learned more about the city and

Capitol Hill than we ever dreamed might be possible: the rooms, the stairwells, the restaurants, the seasons of the year. And we watched as our conference participants grew from hesitant to confident to fully engaged in the governing process, both back home and in D.C. We are grateful for those experiences.

We also watched the struggle that ensued each time our participants realized their own differences of opinion, springing from long held and deeply felt convictions. As we watched those struggles and kept up with current events, we could not help but be aware of a growing polarization in our country – a polarization matched with a corresponding decline in civil behavior throughout our society. Then one night on the evening news we saw one senior Congressman spit at another, and we decided something had to be done.

We spent two years looking for an organization that would address these concerns on a grassroots level in a way we envisioned. When we didn't find one we stepped in to fill the need and launched the Institute. It has been an incredible journey thus far – one that within the pages of this book we invite you to become a part of. We have learned, we have stumbled, we have grown, and we have blazed new paths.

When our friend Donna Bowling offered to help put our story in writing, we were both humbled and grateful. Working together with her has brought us much joy and fellowship. Translating our experiences to the written page has stretched us and blessed us, and we are deeply grateful to Donna for her patience in working with us. We truly cannot find the words to adequately express our thanks to our families. Jack and Robert Dahnke, and Lucas and Levon Spath have contributed to this effort in countless ways. Without their love and support this could not possibly have happened. We want to extend a special thanks to Sarah Spath who reviewed the manuscript; to our congregations; and to all of those who have journeyed with us, believed in us, encouraged us and supported us. You know who you are. This is your story, too. May our numbers only grow………..

Rev. Cassandra Dahnke and Rev. Tomás Spath

PART 1: THE PROBLEM

"Even the idea of compromise has been compromised, made to sound like weakness, or irresolution. And the result, I fear, is that our public debates, which used to involve a certain amount of mutual yielding, are becoming the civic equivalent of road rage. Can't we do better than that?"
- William Raspberry

We believe there are two problems threatening the strength of our governing process today. One is the lack of civic participation at every level of government, from neighborhood associations to Congress. There is a strong sense of apathy in the air. The other is what we perceive to be a growing polarization in our society along lines of race, socio-economic groups, religion, age, and special interests. We believe that a society that experiences both polarization and low civic participation is a society at risk.

We the people of this United States of America have become a nation divided against ourselves. In place of the "more perfect union" envisioned by those who hammered out our Constitution at the original Constitutional Convention, we find ourselves plagued by division of our people into groups whose membership often appears determined solely by narrow self-interest. Unrestrained self-interest that is blind to the needs of the larger community is damaging the fabric of our common life.

Voices urging a more generous approach to our common problems are like those crying in the wilderness. They cannot be easily heard in the general cacophony that surrounds us in the public square--that space where we come together as the people of this national community to seek solutions. This is the place where we have historically engaged the problems that beset us internally, and where we address the challenges posed by external enemies who assail us. The public square includes media talk shows, newspapers, government and other public forums, the Internet, private meetings and personal conversations. Because no single individual or group has control of the truth, we need the public space to hear other voices than our own in order to seek a more perfect truth.[1]

2

As we seem to splinter into increasingly narrow enclaves, a decline in the tone of our interactions with fellow citizens has contributed to a general sense of demoralization, if not crisis, in our common life. The tone has become especially acrimonious in discussions with those with whom we disagree. In candid moments some of our public servants express anger and grief as they share the substance of their daily interactions.[2] As the fault lines running through our political, religious and personal lives widen, we feel an ever-increasing sense of urgency and disquietude. Can the rumblings we hear and feel portend the disintegration of the common foundation on which we stand as a nation and as a people?

There seem to be few places at present where true dialogue about issues affecting us as a nation is possible.[3] Our growing uneasiness with the state of discourse in our national civic life is reflected in ever more frequent and urgent calls for a return to civility in all our interactions, but especially in our encounters in the public square.[4] Perhaps in our growing anxiety over the current state of our national communal life we are at last coming to fully understand the bedrock truth beneath the eloquent Preamble to our Constitution. For unless we are capable of envisioning and continuing to seek "a more perfect union," we will be incapable of establishing justice, insuring domestic tranquility, providing for the common defense, promoting the general welfare, or securing the blessings of liberty to ourselves and our posterity.[5]

Politics at its most basic is nothing more than the way we conduct ourselves in an organized fashion in our human society.[6] Living in community as social beings requires a delicate dance of give and take as we work out solutions to common problems. Too many of us have forgotten--or worse, have never learned--the steps to that dance. When the public square is full of little more than shouted diatribes and dialogue becomes impossible, our democratic society is in danger, and our survival as a civilized society is in peril.

When we cannot engage each other across the varied spectrum of our beliefs in respectful dialogue that seeks common solutions to difficult issues, we lose the enrichment available from a variety of viewpoints. When we talk and interact only with like-minded citizens, we risk our beliefs becoming ever more extreme as our positions, constantly reinforced and never challenged, become like pilings set in concrete. At that point we are in danger of demonizing those who dare to express beliefs different from the ones to which we stubbornly cling.

3

Our greatest peril comes when we demonize each other to such an extent that we lose sight of our common humanity. When we fail to see sisters or brothers in the faces of those with whom we vehemently disagree, treating them as less than human becomes a real possibility. We become like passengers at opposite ends of the ship of state, ready to destroy the very vessel we inhabit rather than make common cause with our brothers and sisters in the opposite end of the boat. If we persist in such an attitude, of course, the entire ship will sink.

Civility in our public square is a necessity if we wish to preserve this democratic nation for our posterity. For the harsh truth is that the opposite of civility is not simply incivility, but the terror and chaos that come with the disintegration of civilized society. A failure to reclaim civility in the public square will lead us relentlessly in that direction.

Fortunately the solution to the current abysmal lack of civility in our political life is easy to state--though difficult to execute. We need look no further than the democratic traditions of spirited discussion and compromise through which our people were forged into one nation.[7] Those who established this country, like us, had very different views of how best to establish the structures that would ensure a future for the new nation. They nonetheless managed to reach consensus on many important issues. In order to do so they had to engage in dialogue with those with whom they disagreed.

No doubt our forebears in this country knew they were attempting something novel in the long history of humanity. They also knew the alternatives from which they had fled seeking freedom. A democratic society in which power resided in the people offered protection for their new freedom. Only by respectful dialogue with each other in the public square can we, who collectively hold ultimate power in this representative democracy, hope to maintain our democratic society and craft solutions to the problems we face. There is no other way to continue this remarkable experiment that has been bequeathed to us.

Let there be no misunderstanding, this book is not about seeking consensus at all costs. Consensus may be necessary in Congress to pass legislation, but it is not necessary for us to dialogue respectfully about difficult issues that affect us all. Some may even consider civility to constitute weakness, insincerity or lack of conviction. With those who feel that way, respectful dialogue may be impossible. This book will make no attempt to offer a thorough and scholarly sociological, psychological, political or theological analysis of our current situation or otherwise explain the growing concern about the uncivil acts which seem ever more prevalent in our society. What this book does offer is a model to show each of us individually how to engage in the type of dialogue necessary for effective interactions at each level of our representative form of government, using the rules that have been developed by the Institute.

This book is also an invitation to others to reflect further on this topic and perhaps offer a more thorough exposition than is possible within the limits we have set for ourselves. What we are offering is simply a call for change in the way we currently interact with each other in the public square. We want to begin the dialogue about how we can more effectively discuss the issues on which we differ. And we offer the tools to make that dialogue possible.

Part of the problem is that we are often afraid to discuss the reasons why we disagree. Perhaps we are fearful that giving voice to our differences will expose just how deep they are. Yet by remaining silent at the points of our differences with others, we can lose the ability to articulate our own thoughts and opinions. We thus render ourselves even less able to explain our convictions when, eventually and inevitably, our differences come into the open.

When we fail to respectfully express our true opinions, we may also find ourselves beset by general feelings of frustration or even rage that can taint all our future encounters with those with whom we disagree. Then instead of speaking our minds with respect for our adversary when we do finally speak up, some of us become venomous or even violent. This book provides a blueprint for changing our ways. Put very simply, there is a problem and it is us. We have the power to change our behavior for the better, and this book outlines how we can do that.

Perhaps the character of the uncivil behavior we currently see demonstrated may be no different from that which has gone before, and may be in some ways less offensive. But the reality is that we are disturbed by it.[8] In the final analysis, whether the current behavior in the public square differs or does not differ from that of the past, the uncivil and inappropriate actions we are currently witnessing in our public square are simply wrong and unacceptable. Recurrent incivility is corrosive to our society and to our democratic process. Our divisive behavior is tearing us apart. Power resides in the people in a representative democracy. It is we who must negotiate with each other over tough issues in order to reach a consensus about how our elected officials should address them. That means, at a minimum, we must be able to engage in dialogue with each other.

From the very beginning of our democracy there has been a concern about civility. The first president of the United States of America, George Washington, wrote and published his own list of rules for civil behavior, *Rules of Civility & Decent Behaviour In Company and Conversation.* [9] We Americans set high standards for ourselves, and we are regularly distressed when our behavior falls short. That does not mean it is wrong to have high standards. Nor does it mean that we must accept the status quo, even though we fallible human beings will always fall short in some ways of the goals that we set for ourselves. Like our desire for community, our failure to achieve perfection, whether in our personal behavior or our democratic society, is also part of our human nature.

Because we are one people living in one national community, each of us has a stake in creating the possibility for authentic dialogue in our public square and each of us shares in the blame when what we see and hear is ineffective. How we talk with each other affects not only the nature of the relationships immediately involved, but also the health of the entire community, just as relationships between individual family members affect the health of the family as a whole.

The uncomfortable truth is that if we are to solve the difficult problems we face as a national community, we must act affirmatively and with courage and clarity to reclaim civility in the public square. Civility is quite simply the glue that holds us together and allows us as citizens of a representative democracy to dialogue with each other. We seem to be spending so much time these days attacking those with whom we disagree that we are losing sight of the real enemies we face in the world. [10]

We also need input from all of those in our wonderfully rainbow-hued variety to reach effective solutions to problems in which each of us is invested. We must engage in effective dialogue about the painful differences we have over tough issues. We also need to learn how to more constructively deal with dissent in this country. We need to react in some fashion other than demonizing our opponents and secretly hoping they will simply go away. Unfortunately, too many of us have progressed from skepticism to outright cynicism about the state of relations in our public square and have tuned out and dropped out of the current fractious political scene. [11]

The following tools for effective participation in the public square while maintaining civility offer the possibility of increasing our participation as well as improving the nature of our interactions in the public square. If you are reading this book, you probably desire a more positive process for tackling the serious issues that beset our society. You may be fed up with uncivil behavior, but have few practical ideas for countering the deluge of corrosive and divisive behaviors. Like many of us you may simply avoid listening or participating in situations where animosity has become all too common. You nonetheless value civility and hunger for any evidence of its presence. If you are one of what we sense is a weary majority, this book with its practical lessons on reincorporating civility in our interactions in the public square is for you.

Much has been written about civility, or more accurately the lack of civility, in our common life in recent years. Books devoted to this topic appear regularly. Many of those books offer wise and helpful advice on personal human interactions: how to relate to co-workers on the job or how to interact safely with impossibly difficult and angry people. This book, however, has a different and more specific purpose. The purpose of this book is to enhance civility in the personal interactions of our common political life. This book offers tools that will allow us to create practical solutions to our common problems. According to Cassandra Dahnke and Tomás Spath, co-founders of the Institute for Civility in Government (referred to in this book as "the Institute"), "Many have studied this issue. Many have proclaimed it. We have lived these rules and found them to work."

The Institute is a membership based, non-profit, 501(c)(3) organization working to reduce polarization in our society by focusing on the very public civility (or lack of it!) in the governing process. The Institute has two priorities. One is to educate people about their role in government and equip them to participate effectively in it. The other is to help government officials, staff, and constituents understand that the manner in which we govern ourselves is often as important as the positions that we take. The founders of the Institute chose to focus on the governing process because 1) it is public 2) it is something in which we all have a stake, 3) it is a venue where change can occur, and 4) it influences other areas of our lives together in community. The Institute does not endorse any political candidate, nor does it take a position on any issue. It is about process, not positions. The Institute facilitates dialogue, teaches respect, and builds civility.

Let us turn, then, to a discussion of the ten rules for fostering civility developed by Cassandra Dahnke and Tomás Spath in their work with the Institute.

PART 2: THE SOLUTION

Rule #1: Know Yourself

"Civility is claiming and caring for one's own identity, needs, and beliefs without degrading someone else's in the process." Rev. Cassandra Dahnke and Rev. Tomás Spath

"I am frankly terrified by the devastating intellectual naiveté illustrated by someone who thinks 'facts' ever come without being defined and interpreted within some conceptual scheme or another. The distinction is not between those who are involved in philosophical reflection and those who are not, but between those who are self-aware and self-reflective and those who are not (i.e., the difference between those who are unwittingly at the mercy of the conceptual scheme which is shaping their interpretation of the world, and those who are aware enough to exercise some degree of deliberate self-reflection and critique)."
- William Greenway, Ph.D., Austin Presbyterian Theological Seminary

We human beings differ from other species in our capacity for self-reflection. We know, for example, that we are vulnerable and that we will die. Our capacity for self-reflection affects who we are and how we live our lives. It also allows us to choose how we grow and change. That means our behavior is potentially less subject to control by others than that of other species. However, we also operate by imitation, not only as children, but also as adults.[12] Consequently, the context in which we grow up and live our lives has an important impact on who we are and how we see ourselves and our world.

In order to live our human lives most fully, we need to be aware both of our capacity for self-reflection and of our habit of imitation. Each of us operates in the context of a frame of reference. Typically that frame of reference is the context into which we are born and in which we mature. Our frame of reference determines our ways of seeing and experiencing the world in which we live. These ways of seeing and experiencing our world are often so ingrained that we do not recognize their impact on our perceptions. Self-reflection allows us to step outside our own frame of reference and experience the world from other perspectives. The ability to engage in this sort of rigorous self-reflection is enhanced when we encounter others who possess different frames of reference. Self-knowledge allows us to benefit more profoundly from our encounters with others who are different from us. Rather than basing our response to them on our habitual ways of interpreting the world, we are more likely to listen to what they have to say and why they are saying it.

In the context of civility in the public square, we must not only know and understand our own frame of reference, but also be aware of how it shapes our own position on any given issue. Self-reflection and the self-knowledge that results can help us understand why we hold a specific position and why we believe our position contributes to the common good. Knowing ourselves well through self-reflection is also important in understanding our motivation for personal involvement, whether that involvement is because of a particular issue or relationship or because of our perception of the system itself.

With a solid foundation of self-knowledge, we are better prepared to enter into dialogue using basic courtesy and good manners, paying attention, listening quietly while someone else is talking, and asking questions about things we do not understand. In this way we have an opportunity to learn about the beliefs, perceptions and prescriptions of those with whom we dialogue. Awareness that what we do not hear may hurt us is helpful in this process. We also need to be aware that we can be disadvantaged by those things we do "hear" if our hearing is colored by our beliefs and perceptions.[13]

Self-knowledge allows us to see how our ways of seeing and experiencing the world are different from those of others. Dialogue with others from whom we differ offers rich possibilities to more clearly define our own frame of reference. The resulting self-knowledge allows us to decide if we want to continue to be guided by our existing frame of reference, or change that frame of reference to one that is better grounded in a new understanding of reality. In either case our efforts at self-reflection coupled with dialogue can help us in our life-long search for self-knowledge.

BELIEFS, PERCEPTIONS, PRESCRIPTIONS

The following story told by Tomás Spath illustrates how our frame of reference affects our beliefs and how our beliefs influence our perceptions and ultimately our actions. This story demonstrates why self-knowledge is a critical first step for effective dialogue with others.

I was awestruck by Dr. Albert Eldrige's presentation at a conference I attended. Dr. Eldridge was chair of the Political Science Department at Duke University. He shared a formula that had an immediate impact on me. He asked: "Why do we have conflicts? What can we do about them? Is there a way to dialogue through our conflicts?" Dr. Eldridge's formula was: One's belief systems influence one's perceptions of things, and one's perceptions in turn influence one's prescriptions. More simply: what you believe influences what you see and what you see influences what you do. As soon as I heard Dr. Eldridge's formula, I thought of a situation in my own life to which his words applied.

I grew up in Argentina. My parents were missionaries in Argentina for the Lutheran Church in America. In my elementary school I learned what I then believed everyone in every school in the world learned: that Argentina was the best country in the whole wide world. I really believed this as a child, and to some degree I still have this perception. Argentina is beautiful. It has everything one would ever need---the ocean, the mountains, valleys, waterfalls, the pampas, the tango, friendships, old world charm, beautiful language, passion---everything. As a child growing up in Argentina, I thought like a typical Argentinean. Therefore I learned to dislike my neighbors, the people of Chile. Why did I learn to dislike the Chileans? The reason, it occurs to me now, was that in my early history classes, I heard all about Don José de San Martín, the George Washington of Latin America. I idolized San Martín, who was born in the town of Yapeyú, Argentina, on Feb. 25, 1778. San Martín enrolled in the Seminary of Nobles in Madrid, Spain in 1786. His father was a lieutenant governor while his mother was a niece of the conquistador of "El Chaco." San Martín is credited with having a good military mind. Since he studied in Spain he had a good grasp of how the Spaniards thought. San Martín liberated the Argentine community from the Spaniards on July 9, 1816. Thereafter he crossed the huge Andes mountain range--not once, not twice, but three times!-- and joined forces with Bernardo O'Higgins, who is now credited by the Chilean people with being the Liberator of Chile.

Based on my beliefs about the superiority of Argentina, I thought I knew better. I thought, as did my compatriots in Argentina, that San Martín was the true Liberator of Chile, but that he had been cheated out of acknowledgement for that by the Chileans. After liberating Chile, San Martín traveled to Bolivia and Peru to also help those countries become free and independent nations. As a child I came to believe that Argentina is a great nation that produces great leaders for whom our neighboring countries owe us thanks. Certainly, I thought, this must be true! I learned it in school from my teachers, and I knew that teachers do not lie. They teach only truth. We in Argentina believed our great leader Don José de San Martín served not only our community, but also other nations by leading us all to our freedom from Spain.

My idealization of San Martín presented a problem when my father returned from an important meeting in Buenos Aires one day. We were living in Azul, Argentina, which was at the time a small town about 300 kilometers southwest of Buenos Aires. I was 13 years old. When my dad came home from his meeting, he reported that the church had asked him to move to Chile to start new churches. When my father asked us how we would like to move to Chile, we kids all exclaimed: No Way!!! As I heard the request I could only think: Who in the world would want to move to Chile when they don't recognize Don José de San Martín as their real liberator from the Spaniards!?! My belief was that the Chilean people were not grateful for the great leader that Argentina had produced and graciously shared with them to liberate all of us from the Spanish conquerors. My perception was that if we moved to this ungrateful country, I would not only live with ungrateful people, but I would also be considered a traitor by my own friends back home in Azul.

I had to devise a way to stop this move. While we were discussing the situation as a family at the dinner table, I thought about having a democratic vote. I asked my dad if we could take a family vote regarding the possible move to Chile. He agreed that it would be a good idea, so after some discussion we voted. I won!!! There were three kids living at our house and two parents so the vote was three against the move and two for the move.

We moved to Chile two months later. I learned that two parental votes hold more power than three children's votes. I still remember how awful I felt as we prepared to move to Chile. To my parents' credit, although we kids did not control whether we moved, we did get control over how we moved. My parents wanted to fly to Chile, but we wanted to see the mountains that our hero struggled to cross when he liberated the Chilean community from the Spaniards. So our parents consented to cross the Andes Mountains by train. And what a trip it was! Every mile of the way I became more convinced of the skill and bravery of San Martín. The trip reinforced my belief that Argentina was the best country in the whole wide world.

From the moment I first laid eyes on the Chileans, I perceived an ungrateful people. They did not recognize the greatness of my hero,

San Martín, so I believed they were lazy, complacent, and irresponsible. My prescription for this situation was to stay away from these ingrates. During our time in Chile I did my best to do exactly that. My best friend in Chile was a kid from Switzerland. We did almost everything together. In my own neighborhood, it was hard to go out and watch others playing soccer, a game I have always truly enjoyed, and not participate. But I stayed away, and I refused to play with the Chilean kids. What a way to build relationships! My own prejudices, fears and beliefs separated me not only from the Chileans with whom I lived, but also from a sport I really enjoyed. It was only years later that I came to appreciate that the Chileans are really very nice people.

What we believe controls our perceptions and often our actions as well. What I learned in Argentina was really not that different from what people learn in other parts of the world. Most of us believe we were born and raised in the best country in the world. Argentineans call it Argentina. Canadians call it Canada. Mexicans call it Mexico. Palestinians call it Palestine. Israelis call it Israel. Those of us who live in the United States often call it "America," by which we mean just the United States of America, and not all of America, which includes all the countries in North, Central and South America. Many people who live in America, but not in the United States, resent the people of the United States for using the term "American" to mean exclusively those who live in the U.S.A., because they perceive that we are all Americans!

What is just as interesting is how we humans perceive the land we call home. When I was growing up in Argentina, my geography lessons taught me all about Las Malvinas, the islands just off the coast of the southern tip of Argentina. The same would be true in almost any classroom throughout South America. Imagine my surprise then when my family moved to Chile, and my geography teacher taught me about the Falklands, the name used by the British (and the Chileans!) to designate that same bit of land off of the Argentine coasts. The British may claim the Falklands, but the Argentines still consider the islands their own. In 1820, four years after San Martín liberated Argentina from Spain, Argentina took control of the islands from Spain. Eleven years later, the United States declared there was no government there, which paved the way for Britain to regain control of the islands some years later. Maps showing these islands located east of the southern part of Argentina are different depending on where they are made.

This same situation is repeated in other parts of the world. Visiting Palestinian refugee centers in Beirut, Lebanon in 1982, I saw in their classrooms a map of the Middle East. The land I learned in Argentina to call Israel, on the Palestinian maps was called Palestine. Once after I made a presentation on world conflicts incorporating the formula I had learned from Dr. Eldridge about beliefs, perceptions, and prescriptions, an American who worked for Shell Oil who had heard my presentation spoke with me. He told me that he had lived in Iraq in the late 1980s. I asked him if he had bought a map of Iraq while living in Iraq, and whether the map included Kuwait. He said he did not know. The next morning I received a phone call from this man, who literally could not believe what he had seen on his map. The schools in Iraq used a map that did not include Kuwait. For the children in Iraq, Kuwait did not exist.

If some children in the world learn that the islands are called Las Malvinas, while others learn they are the Falklands, and for some Israel is called Palestine, while others learn it is called Israel, it is no wonder we have problems communicating when we reach adulthood. Perhaps a more civil way to learn would be to teach all of our children the various names each land has. But in order to teach our children effectively, we have to understand our own belief systems and where they come from, and we have to be aware that our beliefs, perceptions and prescriptions are our own, and not universal throughout humanity. Will this in itself eliminate conflict? No, but it is an initial first step.

Rev. Tomás Spath

To know ourselves, to have a deep self-understanding, is a requirement for engaging others with civility. Otherwise our beliefs will color our perceptions and our actions in ways we may not fully understand. As Tomás' story illustrates, we each grow up within a particular frame of reference that informs our beliefs and ultimately affects our interactions with others. While it is possible to step out of our own frame of reference long enough to evaluate whether or not it accords with reality, doing so requires hard work and a willingness to risk changing our own perception of reality. Hard work and a willingness to be open to change are skills that serve us well when we seek to enter into dialogue with others. But before we can truly hear the beliefs and opinions of others, we must know where we ourselves stand

and why. When we stand on that firm foundation of knowledge of ourselves, we are better equipped to hear others without feeling threatened when their beliefs are different from our own.

As we relate to our elected officials and to others with whom we engage in political dialogue, we need to be aware of our own belief systems, and the larger systems from which our beliefs are taken. To attempt to influence another person requires knowing where that other person stands and then seeking ways to convey our own perceptions to help build understanding from which solutions may be sought to common problems. Such mutual understanding is not an easy goal, and without the foundation of self-awareness it may be impossible to reach.

Rule # 2: Listen with Your Strength

"Wisdom is made up of ten parts, nine of which are silence."
Author unknown

Listening is a conscious effort to hear by attending closely to what another person is saying.[14] Synonyms include: concentrating, focusing, or keeping your mind on, paying heed and taking notice. Each of these is an action requiring considerable energy. Too often listening is characterized as a passive activity when this could not be further from the truth. Listening well is a high-energy exercise of ears, mind, and heart. It requires our full attention and the kind of total focus that is exhausting if carried out over an extended period of time. Just ask a lawyer whose job requires listening to witnesses in a trial, a physician who must seek complete and accurate information in order to care for a patient, a teacher who must discern the best way to teach a particular student, or a faithful pastor whose job includes conversations with distressed parishioners.

Listening well requires attention to the simple rules of courtesy we were taught as children. In order to truly listen we need to be quiet when someone is talking to us and not interrupt until they are finished. Listening cannot be done while multitasking. We cannot listen while playing, working or surfing the Internet. Truly listening means putting all of our energy into hearing what the other person is trying to communicate--in other words, listening with our strength.

Listening with our strength also requires more than just attention to the words being said. Attentiveness to what is not being verbalized, but is nonetheless part of the communication, requires listening carefully for what lies beneath the words.[15] Thus we need to continually ask ourselves as we listen: What is being said? How is it being said? Is the speaker talking loudly or softly? What tone of voice is being used? Is it soothing or demanding, engaged or distant? What does the tone communicate? Is the person angry or joyful, confused or full of conviction? Is the information coming quickly and smoothly, or is there hesitation? What is the person not saying? Listening means watching the other person carefully while making eye contact if possible. Communication includes much more than the words we say. Body language and that indescribable something that comes through the eyes alone are often just as important as the words we hear.

Listening well requires time, a real challenge in our fast-paced society. Time spent listening with our strength is a precious gift to others. Dietrich Bonhoeffer said listening is "the first service that we can perform for anyone."[16] Listening with our strength means giving our time, our energy, and our complete attention to another person. When we do, we may be surprised by what we hear and by how much we can learn about our partner in dialogue. Hope blossoms when people allow themselves time to slow down and engage in conversation.[17] Listening with all we have to offer is the true beginning of authentic interaction with others. Listening is a way to value another person. [18] In our society each of us has the right to speak our concerns. True civility requires that we listen with our strength when someone offers us the gift of a look into their heart and soul and mind. Listening with our strength demonstrates our commitment to civility.

LISTENING WITH YOUR STRENGTH MAKES A POWERFUL IMPRESSION

The following story from Cassandra Dahnke and Tomás Spath illustrates the power of listening with your strength.

Although many people feel they have no voice in the governing process, our experience working with people through the Institute has been different.[19] If you want a good example of listening with your strength, just watch a Congressional legislative aide or staff person in action. Congressional staffers are models of how to listen with your strength. As much as they would like to, members of Congress do not have enough time to meet with every interest group or every constituent who wants to communicate with them and still have time left to do their job of representing all of their constituents. Each member of Congress is only one person and must therefore rely heavily on legislative staff for these activities. The staff people are trained by the members of Congress who hire them to listen well, because the members are interested in hearing what individuals or groups have to say about issues before Congress.

These staff members are usually highly motivated, intelligent, and educated people. Most of them are also extremely good listeners. Congressional staffers generally provide their undivided attention to those with whom they are meeting. When a constituent visits, they bring a pad and pencil and listen with their full attention. They make good eye contact, they ask questions to clarify information, and they take notes. They have to listen with their strength because it is their responsibility to provide their member of Congress with as much helpful information as possible on all of the legislation to which they are assigned. One key piece of information is how constituents and special interest groups feel about that legislation.

While we have met with many Congressional staff persons through the years who have listened to us extremely well, one exceeded all reasonable expectations. During the seven years we led legislative conferences for Texans in Washington, D.C., we met on each trip with a member of Senator Kay Bailey Hutchison's staff. For many years that staff person was Shelby. Through the years, Shelby got to know us and our groups. She knew we were always a politically diverse bunch of folks, and that different people made the trip each year. She came to expect us to have position statements on a number of issues, and she expected different people from the group to speak regarding each piece of legislation. We knew she listened graciously, listened well, and asked good questions. We trusted her to take our message back to the Senator. We just did not realize at first how she truly listened with her strength, and the advantages that would provide her in her powers of recollection.

One year the group we took to Washington was particularly concerned about a pending tax bill, but after much hard work and dialogue they had to agree they could not reach sufficient consensus to offer a position on the bill to their congressional representatives. Nonetheless, they went to Senator Kay Bailey Hutchison's office as usual. There they advised the Senator's amazed staffers that while the group had not reached a consensus on the tax bill, they did agree on three questions about which they wanted further information. Senator Hutchison's staffers paid close attention, as always, to what the group had to say and who said it.

One year later, some of the same people returned and had again reached consensus on some of the issues they had discussed. As usual, when we arrived at the Senator's office, we were ushered into a large conference room. As many as were able sat at the massive table that nearly filled the space, while others stood around the perimeter of the room, taking in the photos on the wall as they waited for a staff person to arrive.

When Shelby arrived, the thirty members of the group began introducing themselves one by one around the room with their name and where they were from. As Kimberly Glaus-Late introduced herself, Shelby immediately stopped the introductions and said, "I remember you! You were here last year and you spoke on ......, and you said...," naming both the issue which Kimberly had presented for the group that had been there the year before, and the position the group had taken. And she was right! The people attending the legislative conference that year were astounded and impressed. Shelby obviously knew how to listen with her strength! This attention to detail provided her with the memories she needed to make an instant connection with the group a full year later, and thus provided a fuller and richer context for the new information she was about to receive.

Rev. Cassandra Dahnke

Once we know ourselves and our own beliefs, we are in a better position to listen to others. That listening will be most effective if we truly listen with our strength. As the above story illustrates, this sort of listening requires complete attention and focused energy. When we enter into dialogue willing and able to focus our total attention on hearing what the other person has to say, the person to whom we are listening will know they are being heard, and that dialogue will be more effective. When we truly hear what another person has to tell us, we also succeed in creating community, however briefly. That is an additional reward for our concerted efforts to listen with our strength.

Rule # 3: Respect: Differences are Enriching

"What we have to do ... is to find a way to celebrate our diversity and debate our differences without fracturing our communities. "
- Senator Hillary Rodham Clinton

America seems to be increasingly divided into groups identified by their uniform mindset. Too many of us have arranged our lives to avoid interactions with those who are different and especially with those who hold different beliefs on issues we deem important. We seek confirmation of our own views by associating with those who never disagree with us on anything of substance. Even our churches are increasingly divided along the political fault lines in our culture.[20] Unfortunately, when we only talk with those who reinforce what we already believe, our views tend to harden and become impervious to change--even when change might mean improvement.[21] As a nation our political leaders and the more activist among us argue unceasingly about values in our public square, something that differentiates us from European countries according to one observer.[22] Some argue that our discussion of values in the public square is part of what characterizes this country, and they see that as appropriate.[23] Others feel that too many of our current discussions in the public square might more accurately be characterized as screaming matches rather than true discussions of value differences.[24]

We express belief in the value of our representative form of government and, in theory at least, the right of everyone to have a voice as we shape government actions. But in practice, listening to those who are different, especially those with opposing views, is a challenge. We also forget that different voices can say the same thing, yet be heard differently. Some people simply "hear" one better than the other, and sometimes the voice of a child can be heard best of all. We need to respect and appreciate the rich variety offered by all kinds of voices in our pluralistic society. Given the wide variety of religious and secular beliefs represented in this country, arguments about values are to be expected. While some use value issues as weapons with which to demonize those with whom they disagree, there are many in this country who see respectful arguments about values as appropriate. They recognize that living in community means learning to get along with those who abide by different values and have different beliefs.[25] The wisest of these practical individuals even recognize that their beliefs can be enriched when considered in light of different perspectives. They are open to the possibility of adjusting their beliefs as a result of conversation with others with whom they initially disagree.

Bonds of commitment to shared values make it easier to dialogue effectively, but the most important values that we can share may be a respect for differences and a willingness to discuss issues in a civil manner in spite of those differences. Those values are necessary to encourage the expression of divergent views by various segments of the society. If groups with divergent views feel they have no voice and that their views are not being represented in the public square, those individuals may simply drop out and cease to make the effort to participate in our representative government through their votes. [26]

A loss of participation across a range of views is damaging to the health of our national community. Some of those who drop out may find themselves susceptible to the violent rhetoric and actions of fringe elements who believe only violence can be truly heard or effect change. Political apathy and lack of commitment to those in authority are early indicators of this danger. Some argue these markers are already evident in this country.[27] Besides the real danger to our national community inherent in a failure to hear the myriad views and values represented in our society, when we fail to encourage expression of different beliefs and values we also lose the rich possibilities that could be ours if we would consider all the views and values available as we seek solutions to common problems.

When we do listen to different views on common problems, our respect for diversity can be our greatest strength because it allows for creative solutions incorporating the best of many perspectives. The United States has long been referred to as the "melting pot" of the world. Whether we have all actually blended as much as some claim is subject to debate, but people of different traditions certainly do live and work side-by-side in this country. We have sampled and appreciated much from each other's heritages in the form of music, food, and art. This is a good beginning. Yet when it comes to the diversity of ideas and philosophies represented in our "melting pot," many of us feel threatened. We seem to draw lines in the sand and refuse to cross them. Enjoying ethnic food is one thing. Seriously considering the thoughts and ideas of the people for whom that food is a beloved tradition is something else entirely.

However, true civility comes when we not only respect the outer trappings of those with different beliefs, but also try to understand the underpinnings of their beliefs as well. Within the framework of our national community where we live side by side, we would do well to learn and understand all we can about others: who they are, how they think and what they hold dear in life. Understanding the different concepts that people have about such topics as family, loyalty, power, control, decision-making, faith and government can enrich us by forcing us to reexamine our own values and belief systems. After such careful examination we will find ourselves with either a more informed commitment to our position or a desire to refine it with understanding gained from the other's perspective.

INDIVIDUALS FROM DIFFERENT BACKGROUNDS ENRICH THE DIALOGUE

The following story from Cassandra Dahnke demonstrates how differences can indeed enrich discussion in unexpected ways.

While I worked at the Presbytery of New Covenant, my responsibilities included providing information to congregations about environmental issues and concerns. As a result, I was invited to attend an interdenominational environmental conference in Washington, D.C. in 1995. The conference was targeted at individuals like me within the church who had experience in environmental advocacy. It included workshops and presentations on various matters including clean water, clean air, and energy and petroleum issues. The last day of the conference was to be dedicated to meeting with members of Congress to advocate church positions on environmental legislation. I was thankful for the opportunity to participate, but I wanted to enrich the dialogue at the conference by including someone who might have a very different perspective from that of members of traditional environmentalist groups. I approached the conference planners about the possibility of bringing a friend with me to this "by invitation only" event; someone who would bring some much needed expertise to the table. Although the conference planners were somewhat hesitant, they agreed.

Convincing Quart Graves to join me was not an easy task. In truth, he was somewhat apprehensive about attending. He seemed like an unlikely participant in an ecology conference as he had been an executive with a major oil company for many years. But Quart agreed to come along, and I am deeply thankful that he did. Initially Quart's fears were confirmed. He was offended by some conference participants who made blanket attribution of anti-environmental beliefs to those with experiences like his own. Such off-the-cuff emotional statements can quickly cause a discussion to become uncivil. When people sink to an emotional level and begin to demonize the opposition, the heated discussion and name-calling that can result makes rational discussion and attempts to find common ground difficult. The environmental conference we attended potentially could have been a text-book example of how name-calling and labeling can put an end to dialogue and mutual respect. Although all of the conference participants shared a Christian perspective, Quart's positions were generally unlike those of the majority of those attending the conference.

Quart had learned from years of dealing with officials of agencies such as the Environmental Protection Agency and local zoning boards in confrontational situations that unless people could negotiate by creating some feeling of common ground and respect for all parties to a dispute, they would only square off and make consensus impossible. From the beginning he was aware of the potential for hostility at the environmental conference because of the comments about organizations such as the one in which he had played an important role and about people who were doing the same kind of work he had done. Quart saw the situation as typical of many occasions in each of our personal and business lives where opposing views are represented. To his credit and that of others who were there, we sought to overcome any potential antagonism by simply getting to know one another a bit, and conversing with each other about our families and other non-controversial topics. We also talked about conference topics where the potential for common ground existed. That made dialogue somewhat easier.

Despite feeling like a bit of an outsider, Quart listened carefully to what the others were saying and responded to their ideas from his different perspective and experience. During a discussion about the federal regulations that force auto manufacturers to produce autos with specific miles per gallon, he observed that a large segment of the passenger car population consisted of pickup trucks and SUVs, which are not subject to the regulations because they are called trucks.

He suggested there should be the same standards for these vehicles as there are for autos, unless they are actually being used for farming or business. He also joined in the discussion about the gasoline tax. Whereas in the U.S. we complain about 60 to 70 cents per gallon in taxes, in Europe the taxes are $3.00 to $4.00 per gallon or even higher in some countries. As a result Europeans think differently about the types of cars they purchase than do most of us in the U.S.A. Quart suggested that if gasoline taxes could be dedicated to addressing environmental issues, it might be useful to advocate higher taxes on gasoline. He also spoke to the other conference participants about alternate energy sources, recognizing as they did that over time we will run out of oil and gas. He agreed with the others there that new sources of energy are harder to find, but the effort must be made. Others at the conference seemed surprised that a former oil company executive could advocate more aggressive development of alternate resources. We all found there were some things we could all agree on, and in fact reach agreement with very little effort once we listened to one another.

Quart found to his surprise that the positions he advocated did not always evoke knee-jerk opposition. In truth, he was seeking the same goals as others at the conference, whether or not they agreed with his approach. People listened politely as he shared positions based on his very different background and experiences. He offered his perspective about how to make changes in the free enterprise system to address environmental issues while taking account of the incentives and disincentives created by various proposals. This was an approach he had used earlier while working with the California Air Resources Board when they were defining fuels under California law. When regulators sought him out at that time because of his energy expertise, he learned that in situations that are approached with an open mind and a desire to seek common ground differences can indeed be enriching. At the environmental conference he shared the knowledge he had gained in previous experiences with other conference participants, and he listened carefully as they shared their perspectives and understandings with him.

Quart likes to think that while he might not have changed many minds that were already made up on the issues we discussed, he was at least able to present a different perspective and perhaps caused other members of the conference to broaden their views and understandings of oil company executives. I found his presence to be a real asset when we left the conference to advocate with members of Congress regarding proposed environmental legislation. While I was well known in the Congressional offices we visited, Quart was an unfamiliar face. While I came at the issues from my faith and my heart, Quart was able to offer scientific and marketing information as well based on his particular expertise. Together we were a more powerful combination than we would have been separately. At the conclusion of the conference Quart gave me a button, which I still have. It reads: "Minds are like parachutes. They only work when they are open." To the open mind, differences are enriching.

Quart Graves

As Cassandra's story demonstrates, different perspectives can enrich dialogue about difficult issues. Individuals with different beliefs than our own can provide us with information not otherwise available. In other words differences are enriching, and our respect for others evidenced in our dialogue with them can help us to take advantage of this reality. When we know our own beliefs and are willing to listen with our strength to the different opinions of others, we not only are able to engage in effective dialogue, but we may also find our own views clarified and enhanced.

Rule # 4: Listen with Your Mind

*"There is one thing in the world which is mightier than all
the hosts of mighty rulers---an idea whose time has come!"*
- Voltaire, French philosopher, historian, dramatist, and essayist

*"Neither party has a monopoly on good ideas. Oftentimes,
the best solutions are crafted from the center."*
- Senator Susan Collins

True listening is not just about being politely quiet while someone
else is speaking. It requires attending with focused, undivided energy.
It also requires us to engage our minds and wrestle with what we are
hearing. Truly engaging in this type of listening offers our respect
to the other person in the conversation. By listening carefully and
demonstrating that we are thinking through what we are hearing, we
show that we value the other person and what he or she is offering.
Just think about how small children respond when we enter into
serious conversation with them and offer respect for their ideas.

While listening with our strength means really hearing what is
being said, listening with our minds means not only hearing, but also
analyzing what is being communicated. By listening with our minds
we also allow for the possibility that we might learn something, and
there is risk in that. We may be forced to reexamine our own views
on a topic of importance to us. In order to listen with our minds we
need to do more than simply pay close attention. As we are listening,
we need to ask ourselves questions such as: Do we understand what
is being said? Are the words clear? Are we focusing all of our energy
on hearing what the other person is saying, or are we just waiting for
them to quit talking so we can speak the response we have already
formulated in our mind?

Sometimes others feel their convictions so deeply, believe in their
positions so strongly, that they cannot imagine the legitimate questions
we might have about what they believe. As we listen we need to help
them understand what they can do to clarify their statements: Do we
ask questions as they come to mind? Do we challenge with respect? Do
we ask for information when we need it--when there is something that
we don't understand, or when a new idea leads us to new thoughts? Do

we acknowledge that we need more background information on the issues being discussed? Are we willing to make the effort to seek out that information and perhaps to learn something new or different? Listening also requires that we discern whether the words that are being said point us towards additional information. Is a teacher guiding us through the printed word, or showing us an example of something? Is a parent pointing out a task that needs to be done, or demonstrating a skill for us? Is a friend or colleague referring us to a website? Are we taking advantage of all the information that is being given to us? Are we following up on referrals? Are we seeking additional facts to inform ourselves further about the topic and to help refine our own views? And finally, when our efforts at the active listening just described are concluded, do we use what we have learned to critically review and refine our own positions?

KNOWLEDGE IS POWER

The following story from Cassandra Dahnke demonstrates how to engage our minds as we listen.

In the previous chapter, I described an interdenominational environmental conference I attended in the mid-1990's in Washington, DC along with Quart Graves, a retired oil company executive. I was invited to participate in that conference because of my work at that time with congregations on environmental inssues.. The conference participants included individuals with much experience in environmental advocacy. We attended a number of workshops and presentations designed to educate us on various energy and petroleum issues. On the last day of the conference we were all to go to various offices in both the U.S. Senate and the House of Representatives to advocate for particular environmental legislation.

One topic on which this conference focused was the appropriateness or necessity of drilling for oil in the Arctic National Wildlife Refuge (ANWR) in Alaska. Those attending the conference were concerned about the potential for damage to the environment if ANWR was opened up for exploration and drilling. This had long been a controversial subject throughout much of the nation.

Debates in the media and the general public about ANWR drilling raged between those who saw the need for increased domestic production of oil and natural gas as most important and those whose primary concerns were the indigenous peoples of Alaska, the natural environment, and the potential for its destruction if drilling were allowed. The group sponsoring the conference and virtually everyone who attended were opposed to drilling for oil in Alaska. To the surprise of many Quart, who had been an employee in the petroleum industry for many years, also expressed his belief that drilling in Alaska was not a necessity at that time.

Just before we were to fan out over Capitol Hill to begin our lobbying efforts, attendees at the conference held a final gathering in a chapel to encourage one another. During that gathering a group of indigenous people spoke. Their people had lived for generations in what is now northern Alaska. Much of their culture and livelihood were tied to the caribou that annually migrated through the land that would be affected if drilling were permitted. They had very real concerns about the development of oil and gas exploration there, and were strongly opposed to opening ANWR reserves for these purposes. People from three generations spoke poignantly of their love for the land and their desires for its protection as well as the preservation of their way of life. Those attending the conference were caught up in the emotions expressed by these individuals. Though the gathering was not a worship service or time of prayer, the chapel setting lent an unmistakable impression of the righteousness of our position.

My own heart was greatly moved by the eloquent and deeply felt pleas for support from these native Alaskans. But I also recognized the gravity of concerns on BOTH sides of the debate. While one middle-aged, indigenous woman spoke, another held up a report of studies that had been done on the issue. The speaker noted that the conclusions from these studies by an independent organization supported the concerns of those opposed to opening ANWR for drilling. As the gathering came to an end, we were asked if we had any questions before taking off to meet with legislators and their staffs. Standing at the very back of the room, I raised my hand and asked if copies of the report displayed by the speakers from Alaska were available for us to share with legislative offices.

While many conference participants quickly turned to stare and angrily demanded to know why I should need any more information to support doing what to them was obviously right, the speaker responded that there were indeed copies of the report available at the front of the room. As I made my way up to the front, the woman who had brought the report received me with a large smile and words of deep gratitude. She handed me several copies of the report and asked if I needed more. She obviously appreciated that I was looking for as much information as possible that might strengthen my position and be considered a resource by legislative offices weighing the pros and cons of proposed legislation on this issue. At the same time, it was disheartening to experience the enmity of other conference participants who passed me on their way out the door and to observe that no one else took advantage of the copies being offered.

Others attending the conference apparently felt that by asking for a copy of the report, I was somehow questioning the legitimacy of the speaker's concerns. The reality, however, was very different. I wanted all the information I could obtain in order to effectively argue in favor of the speaker's concerns. When Quart and I visited legislative offices that afternoon and offered the report to the Congressional staffers with whom we met, they were very appreciative. As much as emotional pleas might touch our hearts and the hearts of our elected representatives as well, it is the responsibility of legislative offices to weigh ALL concerns as they are making their decisions. Information from a wide variety of sources can only broaden their perspective and better inform the difficult decisions that must be made.

During the time when my colleague, Tomás Spath, and I were accompanying fellow church members to Washington, D.C. for briefings and meetings with their Congressional representatives, we began each journey by providing extensive information on the issues that were being discussed in Congress at that time. Participants were given position papers and statements by their church's governing body and other agencies on issues of interest to the group. Once in Washington, the group met with various experts for briefings on the issues they had designated as their focus.

All of this information gave these church members confidence and exceptional influence when they met with their Congressional representatives. They were able to speak specifically about legislation that was being considered. For example one might say, "I have these concerns about this particular piece of legislation" rather than speaking in generalities, such as "I want to end world hunger." The practice of thoroughly researching all sides of relevant issues continues to inform the processes used by the Institute at its conferences and workshops. Listening with your mind requires making the effort to obtain information from a wide variety of resources to be truly informed and effective.

Rev. Cassandra Dahnke

Knowing ourselves and our own beliefs is a first step in engaging in dialogue. When we have established that foundation, we are better equipped to listen with our strength and with respect both to those with whom we agree and to those with differing perspectives. Those perspectives can clarify and enhance our own beliefs. Truly respecting others' perspectives as well as our own, however, requires that we engage our intellect as we listen. Listening with our minds means using them to enrich our own perspectives with all available information. Such thoughtful listening greatly amplifies the value of what we can learn in dialogue with others. As we ask questions and struggle with what we hear, we are able to incorporate what is of value and leave behind what is not.

Rule # 5: Help Comes from the Most Unexpected Places

"Go and speak to your enemies. [But know that] you cannot change someone else unless you first change yourself."
- Nelson Mandela, former President of South Africa

"Tact is the knack of making a point without making an enemy."
- Sir Isaac Newton

We humans are unique individuals and social beings who function best in a communal context. At the same time we are also fallible beings who rarely achieve perfection. These realities mean that we often find ourselves in disagreement with other members of our community. We are in fact likely to encounter individuals with whom we disagree more often than not on issues of importance to us. Disagreeing most of the time, however, does not mean that we will disagree on everything. Rarely is one individual wrong on every issue. Just as rarely is any one individual right on every issue. Thus, there are likely to be times when we will find ourselves on the same side of an important issue as individuals with whom we have previously vehemently disagreed, perhaps on almost every other issue of importance to us. There are also likely to be times when we will simply need the assistance of someone with whom we have disagreed repeatedly in the past.

In the business world we hear this reality expressed in the saying, "Don't burn your bridges." Wise employees leaving an employer are especially cognizant of this counsel. And wise students who may need a reference from a professor who has not been a favorite are well served when they heed the same advice. In politics the equivalent expression would be "An enemy today is an ally tomorrow." This phrase may appear to be the epitome of hypocrisy, the genesis of much cynicism, the death knell of integrity. But in our representative system of government, consensus must be reached on issues of importance in order for concrete action to occur. The reality is that politicians will certainly need to work with someone with whom they have disagreed in the past in order to accomplish an important goal. Their recognition of this truth is critical to successfully performing their jobs.

On Capitol Hill in Washington, D.C. and in state and local governments, people who have fought each other throughout an election must set their differences aside when the votes have been counted if the best interests of all the people are to be served. They must renew their ties as colleagues if they are to work for all of those whom they represent, including those who did not vote for them. This reality is an essential, practical, and unique requirement of our democratic form of government. Indeed, the peaceful transfer of power is the hallmark of our democracy. It requires bravery, trust, and the willingness to forge alliances, however fragile, in order to work together toward the common good.

We see this dynamic at work each year around Election Day and during inaugural ceremonies. We see it in more sober circumstances as the solidarity exhibited in times of war or national crisis. This same principle is at work in the day-to-day business of the governing process. Legislators who agree on very little, who indeed cancel each other's votes on nearly every issue, almost always find some causes on which they not only agree, but also must work together if they are to reach their own important goals. One mundane example at the national level would be the consensus required among many representatives, who otherwise differ on more volatile issues, in order to approve and fund such public works as highway development and road maintenance.[28]

Other issues of importance beyond these more routine and obvious examples of necessary cooperation, however, from time to time bring colleagues together. There are times when people traditionally opposed to one another set aside their differences and engage in a mutual effort to reach an important goal. To those less familiar with the necessary ground rules for our representative democracy, this rule for civility might make our representatives seem hypocritical. We might worry that their alliances are as shallow as the next day's agenda and that they have no greater policy or moral underpinnings than which way the political winds are blowing on a given day. In reality, however, this basic rule for political interaction operates as an incentive for making civility the ground rule for all interactions.

We are creatures of community, and our best achievements are a reflection of that. Even such talented individuals as Lance Armstrong, the great Texas cyclist, do not achieve supremacy on their own. Armstrong was able to triumph because of the support he has received from many people, including his talented and dedicated teammates in each race. The same is true in government. Our greatest legislation, our loftiest goals, and our best demonstrations of government by the people come when our elected representatives are able to make the process work together. Practically speaking, there are pieces of legislation or local community projects that pass by the narrowest of margins, and sometimes unlikely alliances are made to insure their success.

In October, 1994, Raymond Smock, the Historian of the U.S. House of Representatives, was asked how partisans who have argued from opposite sides on tough issues manage to work together after particularly difficult and acrimonious debates. Mr. Smock responded that often those who engage in the most spirited debates on the floor of the Congress are friends and get along well on other issues aside from politics. As Mr. Smock explained, the members know that there will be other battles and an opponent on one piece of legislation may be your ally on the next. It is a rare member who wants to permanently alienate those members of their own or the opposite party with whom they will surely have to work in the future.[29]

It is much easier to seek and to receive someone's help and guidance when we have treated them with respect in the past, even when we have had very real differences of opinion. As the old saying goes, you never know whom you will meet on your way down, so it is best to step carefully on your way up. Or, as one Congressional staffer said, you attract more bees with honey than you do with vinegar. Even this, however, seems to reflect nothing more than practical self-preservation. What the Institute for Civility in Government seeks to encourage is the understanding that we are ALL at our best when we are most civil. That sort of behavior will make our true enemies few, and our true allies many.

OPPOSITES WORKING IN CONCERT MAKE A POWERFUL IMPRESSION

The following story from Tomás Spath describes a remarkable pair of "enemies" working together on issues of importance to both.

Human beings are like onions. Just as an onion is made of layer upon layer, there are layers and layers and layers of truths in each of us. To discover these truths, one must proceed cautiously, intentionally, and with great respect to arrive at the awesome reality of the inner being of another person. Each conversation and each encounter, if handled with sensitivity and genuine respect for the value of the other person, allows a closer approach to the center of their uniquely beautiful reality. This is as true of our enemies as it is of our friends. In fact the effort required to truly get to know an "enemy" may result in seeing the "other" more appropriately as a fellow human being with individual strengths and weaknesses. Perhaps in appropriate circumstances an enemy may even become an ally, in spite of very real differences over other issues of importance.

The Presbytery of New Covenant, a regional governing body of the Presbyterian Church U.S.A., is centered in Houston, Texas. Its offices were once located on the property of the First Presbyterian Church. As the congregation of First Presbyterian Church continued to grow, the congregation found they needed extra space for their youth and educational activities. As a result, the Presbytery needed to relocate its office. Bud Skinner, a retired business man and member of First Presbyterian Church, had some buildings that he wished to sell, and the Presbytery bought one of his properties for their new office.

I was hired by the Presbytery of New Covenant to be the Associate General Presbyter for Justice and Compassion. In that role I helped establish the "Church in Washington," a program that offered Presbyterians annual trips to Washington, D.C. during which they met with their elected representatives in Congress. Bud Skinner heard about this work and became very concerned about the church using his former building to promote political activity. Mr. Skinner was also concerned that the church was "lobbying" for causes with which he did not agree. He was in his 70s at the time and was quite set in his views. One day he paid an unannounced visit to my office. As he appeared at my door he asked nervously, "Are you the one who is responsible for these Church in Washington trips?" He paced back and forth outside my office, refusing at first to come in, and vehemently insisting from his position in the hallway that the church should not be involved in advocating positions to the government.

During the annual Church in Washington trips to Washington, D.C., members of the group shared with their Senators and Representatives consensus opinions hammered out by the group as a whole on issues of importance. Our commitment to the groups that went was that we would present only statements with which each member of the group agreed. Each year reaching such consensus was extremely difficult. People felt passionately about the issues. Each year we told them not to give up their position just to get along, because then the group's position would lack integrity, and they as individuals would go away either disappointed or angry. These people had invested too much time, energy, and resources in these trips for that to be acceptable.

The groups were involved in much study and dialogue, both before and during the trip, but on each trip we generally managed to reach consensus on specific legislation concerning numerous issues. On those occasions when the group was unable to come up with a consensus statement, the group would simply agree to ask the Congressional offices specific questions about the topic under discussion in order to obtain further information for possible consensus in the future.

I explained this whole process to Mr. Skinner as he paced up and down that day outside my office, nearly wearing a trail in the carpet, but my explanation did not seem to help much. The obvious first step was to get Mr. Skinner to enter my office. He finally consented with caution and obvious reluctance. As I invited him in, I explained in more detail how our groups reached consensus on what to say to the Congressional offices with which we met during our trips. As Mr. Skinner relaxed somewhat, I invited him to join us on our next trip. "Come and see for yourself," I said. To his enormous credit he agreed to think about this.

It took several days for him to reach a decision, during which I stayed in contact, answering each of his concerns as they arose. I truly wanted him to experience the relationship-building process we used to reach consensus in our group's work with the Congressional offices of the greater Houston area. To further encourage Mr. Skinner, and in recognition of his heartfelt concerns about this work of the church, I promised that after accompanying us on the trip, if he still felt what we were doing was inappropriate or unproductive work for the church, I would work with him, within the Presbytery, to eliminate this program. With that agreement, Mr. Skinner signed up to be a participant on our next trip.

As this trip approached, my colleague, Cassandra Dahnke, and I were nervous ourselves. We were willingly taking along a participant who could eventually kill a program to which we were strongly committed. Mr. Skinner expressed his concerns about the Church in Washington program to the group. Of course many others in the group disagreed. Otherwise, they would not have been participating. The result of Mr. Skinner's expression of concern about the whole concept of the Church in Washington was much murmuring, some dissension and ultimately a lot of discussion.

We were nervous when this trip began that, because of Mr. Skinner's vocal expressions of concern and disagreement with other members of the group, the trip might end up being of no value at all. However, we learned that dialogue truly can take place between people of good will who disagree. In fact, because of Mr. Skinner's presence, we engaged in group discussions that enlivened the hearts of all who participated. People shared their heart-felt beliefs as they expressed their reasons for participating in the Church in Washington, and explained why they felt the program was not only appropriate, but also of great value to themselves, to their congregations, and to the Presbyterian Church in general.

To our surprise, on this trip Mr. Skinner ended up advocating against funding for the Western Hemisphere Institute for Security Cooperation (WHISC), formerly know as the School of the Americas. This facility, long opposed by liberals, is operated by the United States Army and is located at Fort Benning, Georgia. Numerous protests over the years have targeted this facility because some who trained at the school have been implicated in instances of human rights abuses, such as the assassination of Salvadoran Archbishop Oscar Romero, the murder of four nuns from the U.S. in El Salvador, and the torture and murder of a U.N. worker in Chile.[30] Mr. Skinner teamed with Ms. Marilyn White, an activist who was as liberal as Mr. Skinner was conservative, in advocating against funding the WHISC.

Ms. White was a seasoned advocate who had a personal perspective on every issue discussed by the group at the legislative conference, but was especially concerned about continued funding of the WHISC. She had written numerous letters protesting the WHISC, had attended peace rallies at its gates, and had studied its history. She had also visited many of the countries in which graduates of WHISC had been involved in civil wars. She had been marching, writing letters, and advocating for the closing of the WHISC for years.

Because of her partnership with Mr. Skinner, Ms. White was able to talk with his Congressional Representative, who was involved with oversight of the WHISC, the issue of most importance to her. In return, in exchange for his advocacy with Ms. White on the WHISC funding issue, Mr. Skinner received her support on an issue in which he had an interest. These "enemies" became allies because they had reached consensus on particular issues of importance to both. One was a man, the other a woman. One was tall, the other short. One wore glasses, the other did not. One was old, the other much younger. Walking through the halls of the Congressional office buildings, they seemed as odd a pair as one might imagine, even without knowing their political differences. Yet they made a powerful impact when they made their joint presentation on these issues. Both later told me how wonderful it had been to have someone with different views with them.

Exactly how this partnership came about is difficult to describe with precision, but one thing is certain: it was sincere. What is apparent is that these two individuals, who under almost every other circumstance would consider one another political "enemies," reached mutual agreement through the process of civil dialogue. The result was a staunch conservative and an equally committed liberal walking together to various Congressional offices to share concerns of importance to both. Such advocacy of a position along with someone from the opposite side of the political divide in this country strengthens the proposals offered immeasurably.

Working through tough issues with someone with whom you disagree in order to present a consensus proposal, also helps you better understand the difficult job our elected officials do each day. You learn that consensus does not have to mean giving up your own position or beliefs. It means finding proposals on which people who disagree on many details can legitimately agree, even if agreement is merely about the questions they believe are important to explore in seeking further information for possible consensus in the future.

After participating in the Church in Washington, Mr. Skinner was so impressed by our work that he became a strong supporter. He invited us to address his Sunday School class at First Presbyterian Church about the Church in Washington. He had begun our relationship wanting to kill the program, but after experiencing it in person, he became an advocate for us and recruited others to join our efforts in Washington. He participated himself in the conference again a few years later. He remained extremely emotional about the experience whenever Cassandra and I saw him, often speaking of his gratitude for the experience with tears in his eyes. He had seen people of good will working together on tough issues. He had learned that civil dialogue can accomplish the seemingly impossible, such as helping "enemies" to become allies, even if only on a few issues.

Conversely, Ms. White confessed after this experience that "perhaps it's true that there is more power in making a presentation to a Congressional office when a member of the opposite political party sits by your side."

Rev. Tomás Spath

When you know yourself and your beliefs well and are able to listen with your strength and your mind to those with different opinions, you will almost always find reasons to respect those with whom you disagree. That respect and the necessity for working together to reach common goals can enable you to work with individuals who in different circumstances might be political enemies. Such a vivid demonstration of community in the midst of differences makes a powerful impression on others and shows that help comes from the most unexpected places.

Rule # 6: Relationship is Everything

"Anything we can do to help foster the intellect and spirit and emotional growth of our fellow human beings, that is our job."
- Fred Rogers, Television personality and Presbyterian Minister

"Unexpected kindness is the most powerful, least costly and most underrated agent of human change."
- Bob Kerrey, former U.S. Senator from Nebraska

When differences arise on issues of importance--a virtual certainty in life and in politics--we will have an easier time keeping those differences in perspective if we know and respect the individuals with whom we differ. Having a relationship with those with whom we may disagree will also increase the likelihood that we will remain civil regardless of policy differences. It is harder to be uncivil to someone we know than to a stranger. This is as true of our interactions in the political arena as it is in other areas of our lives, whether our interactions involve our fellow citizens or contacts with our elected representatives. Having a relationship with others, including our elected representatives, can also give us the insight and experience to be more creative in our approach to particular issues on which we wish to be heard. The benefits of a relationship with those with whom we disagree will only be possible, however, if we are willing to engage with one another despite differences on issues of importance, while still valuing the integrity of the relationship more than the results achieved on a particular issue. While even strong relationships do not guarantee agreement on issues, they do by their very nature influence the way we approach issues. Solutions forged in the midst of disagreement have the potential to be far more effective and far reaching than those created out of one perspective alone.

It is in the nature of being human that individuals listen more readily to those they know and trust than they do to strangers or enemies. Therefore having an established relationship built on trust and mutual respect often makes the difference when we seek to be heard by those with whom we disagree on an issue of importance to us, whether they are fellow members of our community or our public servants. Relationships of this caliber do not happen overnight. They require as much work as relationships in our private lives. But just like personal relationships, relationships forged with others through mutual participation in the governing process can be powerful, lasting, and rewarding.

If, on the other hand, we treat those with whom we disagree, including elected officials and their staffs, as pawns to be used to advance our own political agenda, it is less likely we will be taken seriously, if indeed we are heard at all. We may even find ourselves treated in a similar manner. We will also have missed a possible opportunity to enrich our lives through valuable relationships with others. Most people are aware when they are being used for someone else's benefit. In this, as in other life experiences, we reap what we have sown. If our approach is to treat those with whom we disagree as objects to be manipulated toward a particular goal, we will be coolly received, as well we should be. Elected officials, as well as those who disagree with us on issues of importance, or who are undecided about their positions, are people just like us. We human beings, as creatures of community, react best to those who treat us well.

Time is a precious commodity for all of us, but it is especially so for elected representatives, who must represent the interests of many individuals and groups in order to do their jobs well. This does not mean we have to offer gifts or contribute to election campaigns in order to be heard by our representatives on issues of importance to us. It does mean we will be more effective and more likely to be heard by others, especially elected officials, if we approach them as individuals with hopes and dreams, hurts and worries, and ambitions and fears. Those with whom we disagree on political issues, including our public servants, have families and homes, co-workers and in-laws, taxes and their own faith journeys. Our elected representatives are not the one-dimensional caricatures that are too often pictured in the media. As fellow members of the human race, others with whom we disagree on political issues, including our elected officials, deserve to be treated as something more than objects to be used to reach our own goals.

Lobbyists are sometimes viewed as unprincipled people motivated by financial gain to focus exclusively on one side of an issue. They are seen as people who develop contacts with political leaders in order to influence their support of the lobbyist's agenda. In reality, any of us who contact our elected representatives to express our views on issues we deem important are acting as "lobbyists" on behalf of a cause. There are many people who have had a broad impact on our public policy through advocacy that was not self-serving, but had only the greater good in mind. One has only to think of the impact of Martin Luther King, Jr. on civil rights or Rachel Carson on environmental issues to realize this truth. To be effective in contacts with our representatives as we seek to further the common good, we must understand that relationships are just as valuable in politics as they are in other areas of human interaction. We can individually help foster civility in the political process if we work diligently to create and maintain effective working relationships with our elected representatives and members of their staffs as well as with those who seek to influence the political process on specific issues of interest to us, whether we agree with their position or not.

If we take the time to become better acquainted with others involved in the political process, including our elected representatives and those who work for them, rather than simply advocating our own narrowly defined agenda, we will find working together much easier. As we become better acquainted with others involved in the governing process, including our representatives and their staffs, we will also learn more about the governing process and how to participate in it more effectively. When we undertake to establish such relationships, however, we should be prepared to be exposed to information that may either strengthen our own convictions, or alternatively force us to modify our opinions. The reality is that when we enter into true relationships with others with whom we disagree, we open ourselves to the risk of change. That risk is more than worth the benefits we will gain in effectiveness and valuable working relationships, to say nothing of personal growth.

Relationships among members of Congress are every bit as valuable as relationships among citizens and relationships of constituents with their elected representatives in our governing process. What happens among members of Congress occurs in the context of relationship, or lack thereof. As with the rest of us, it is easier for members of Congress to be uncivil to those they do not know. In the current climate in Congress it is difficult for individual representatives to become acquainted with other members of Congress, much less develop working relationships with them. There are a number of reasons for this. In years past, members of Congress spent more time in Washington, D.C. and less time in their Congressional districts. Although there were some extended recesses that allowed for significant travel and time away, most members stayed in Washington, D.C. as long as Congress was in session. That meant that they had many evenings and weekends there. The extra time allowed for social opportunities and provided a venue for members to relax and learn more about one another than the minimal information required to meet the immediate needs of passing legislation, or the reputation portrayed through the media.

Those opportunities for social interaction have become more and more infrequent. Many, perhaps even a majority, of the members of Congress now stay in Washington, D.C. only for the three or four days each week when Congress actually has votes scheduled. On the long weekends they fly home to their districts, and often to their families. There have been some efforts by some members of Congress to address this situation by putting together a bi-annual, bi-partisan retreat for members and their families. The idea was that it would be easier for members of Congress to get acquainted as individuals if their spouses and children were with them. In addition, the organizers believed that members who knew each other in this way would be in a better position to work together in a collegial manner. These retreats have met with some success. Yet while they started out strong, participation has dwindled each year, to the point that it is questionable whether or not they will be continued. The overall lack of time to forge relationships among members has no doubt contributed to a less civil climate on Capitol Hill. We can individually foster civility by encouraging our elected representatives to develop relationships with those of differing political views and for rewarding them with our encouragement, praise and votes when they do so.

In Washington, D.C. you will hear the value of relationships expressed in discussions about trust--as when an individual says, "I trust this person and when she says something, you know you can trust what she says." There is no higher recommendation in Washington, especially when such a recommendation crosses party lines. For that kind of trust to develop, however, relationships must be fostered. When those with opposing viewpoints are engaged in dialogue over a difficult issue, a relationship that insures trust in the other person is invaluable. That relationship can allow each person to believe the other will act in good faith while both try to work through differences.

RELATIONSHIPS AS BOTH SEED AND FRUIT OF STUDENT FORUMS

The following story from Cassandra Dahnke illustrates the value of fostering good relationships in the political arena. The story also demonstrates how relationships can be built, including relationships between members of Congress. The story shows how civility can be enhanced--one relationship at a time.

The Institute teaches individuals how to engage in civil dialogue. The Institute also provides opportunities for members of Congress to get to know one another in a collegial fashion while their constituents engage them in discussions about important issues. This happens when two members from opposing political parties come together for one of the Institute's Congressional Student Forums. At each student forum sponsored by the Institute, either Tomás Spath or I will open by spending a few minutes talking about the importance of civility. We then introduce the members of Congress and tell the students where they're from, how long they have been in Congress, what committees they serve on, what school they graduated from and something personal about themselves such as their favorite music. The Congressional representatives do not make opening statements. They are there to answer questions. After this brief introduction, the students are then free to ask anything they like, as long as they do so with civility and respect. Each Congressional Student Forum lasts an hour and a half, with some additional time afterwards for members of Congress to meet and greet students informally. Participating in a forum, therefore, requires a substantial time commitment.

One reason the Institute for Civility in Government is able to convince members of Congress to participate in Congressional Student Forums is because Institute members have maintained good relationships with their own Congressional representatives. The co-founders of the Institute and many of its members have built those relationships as much out of genuine interest in their representatives as individuals as out of concern for what those representatives might help them do. They have not sought out representatives in order to use them for what they could help accomplish. Building relationships ideally is not a technique or a gimmick just to get what you want from another person, but a way to become a friend and resource to others. In return for their participation in these student

43

forums, members of Congress are provided with an opportunity not only to interact with their constituents, but also to become better acquainted with the members of the opposing party who participate.

With increasing frequency, the Institute is scheduling student forums with Congressional representatives with whom we have not worked before, often based solely on the recommendations of representatives who have been previously involved in one of our student forums. Arranging time on the schedule of a busy Congressperson is a difficult challenge, and our contacts with some members allow them to recommend us to other members. Acting on such a recommendation is an example of real trust based on an existing relationship. For example, Representatives Kay Granger and Mel Watts each agreed to participate in a student forum purely on the recommendation of other members of Congress. Knowing that we came to her on Representative Bill Archer's recommendation, Representative Granger simply told her staff to do whatever we asked when we arrived at her office to discuss arrangements for the student forum. This is an astounding expression of trust in Washington, D.C. Representative Watts also agreed to do a student forum based on the recommendation of Representative Sue Myrick. Representative Myrick had heard us speak in Washington, and decided to recruit Representative Watts, a member of the opposing party, to participate in one of the Institute's student forums with her.

Representative Granger participated with Representative Charles Stenholm in a student forum sponsored by the Institute at Texas Christian University in Ft. Worth, Texas. These two members of Congress worked until 2:30 A.M. the morning of the forum as Congress finalized and voted on that year's budget. Our forum was scheduled to begin in Fort Worth at 11:00 A.M. Both representatives stayed in Washington to vote on the budget. Then, after just a few hours of sleep, they each got on a plane in Washington, D.C. at 7 a.m. and flew to Texas for the student forum. As they walked together into the building where the forum was to take place, they greeted us warmly, and then asked for what they needed most at that moment - a cup of coffee! They were obviously committed to doing the forum.

While they were understandably exhausted, both Representatives shared how refreshing it had been to have time to visit and get to know one another better, not only on the plane, but also for another 40 minutes in the car they shared on their way to the university. While all of our forums don't offer quite that same experience, Representatives can count on some private time before the event, and occasionally after, to get to know one another and to foster a deeper collegial relationship. Such relationships have the potential to make all the difference when seeking common ground and understanding on difficult issues and specific legislation. At the forum with Representatives Stenholm and Granger, one student asked how members of Congress get along on Capitol Hill. Representative Granger explained that upon first arriving on Capitol Hill she and other freshmen Representatives were told they would have an orientation on such practical matters as how to get a phone installed, what supplies were available and the budgets for their offices. Representative Granger was amazed to learn there were two separate orientations for new members of Congress, one for members of each party. (We understand that policy has since changed). She expressed her concern that division and polarization are becoming institutionalized in Congress.

Institutionalized division of members of Congress from the moment they arrive in Washington, D.C. does not allow for the development of relationships that can breed the kind of trust that is essential for dialogue about, and collaboration on, tough issues. There are members of Congress who view polarization and division as a good thing and any attempt to share perspectives in a civil fashion with members of the opposition party as inappropriate. In our experience, however, most members are eager to encourage civility in their interactions with their fellow members of Congress. Still, only demands by both citizens and members of Congress for greater civility in our governing process are likely to create the momentum needed for the kinds of institutional changes that will allow for the building of relationships among members of Congress and for greater civility in their interactions.

Relationships between those who disagree enhance civility. It is harder to be uncivil to someone you know. Building such relationships, however, requires time and the hard work required to know ourselves and truly listen to others, especially those with whom we disagree. We must also value the relationship more than possible short term gains on any one issue, no matter how important.

Rule # 7: Listen with your Heart

"Great ideas, it has been said, come into the world as gently as doves. Perhaps, then, if we listen attentively, we shall hear amid the uproar of empires and nations a faint flutter of wings, the gentle stirring of life and hope."
- Albert Camus

"True peace is not merely the absence of some negative force--tension, confusion, or war; it is the presence of some positive force----justice, good will and brotherhood."
- Dr. Martin Luther King, Jr.

Listening with your strength is a discipline. Listening with your mind is hard work. Listening with your heart, however, is where transformation occurs. Even when an idea makes sense it can be difficult to consider that idea seriously on its own merits if it originates from someone you dislike or with whom you usually disagree. An even greater challenge comes when you begin to understand such an idea and acknowledge that it has possibilities, especially if it goes against your current position on the issue in question. However, the reality is that if we are unwilling to be open to new or different ideas, regardless of their source, we risk losing real opportunities to broaden our understanding and discover possibilities we have not previously considered. Sometimes we believe that accepting anything an adversary says either makes us appear weak, or weakens our own position, or both! Yet true listening includes a willingness to consider the positions of others with whom we disagree. It means opening ourselves emotionally so we become vulnerable to the possibility of having to change our opinions--to the possibility that we may even have a change of heart.

Entertaining the ideas of others does not mean we must let go of our own convictions. But it does mean we must be willing to hear challenges to our beliefs and to develop the ability to articulate the reasons for those beliefs. Truly listening to another so completely that we open our hearts to understand as much as we are able can help us understand the other person's convictions. Such challenging emotional work, however, is tough and scary business. Once we understand not only the mechanics of another person's position, but also the heart of the person behind the position, respect or empathy often follows. That means we now have a relationship with this person with whom we disagree. The reward for such emotional openness is the realization that we and our sometime adversary now exist in community with each other. And that is worth the risk and effort.

ADVOCACY THAT WORKS: CONNECTING WITH THE HEART OF THE LISTENER

The following story from Tomás Spath demonstrates both the challenge and the power of listening with your heart.

Since coming to live in the United States I have always believed that it was important to be in contact with my representatives in Congress. I wrote to my representatives when I lived in Nebraska, New Jersey, Illinois and New Mexico. I continue to write to them now that I live in Texas. I have been told if you want your representatives to listen to your comments, you should pick one or two issues carefully rather than write about numerous issues. As a missionary child who was raised in Argentina, I have a special place in my heart for Latin American countries. It was there, after all, that my life began. It was there that my world views were shaped. Because of this I focused on the issue of U.S. military aid to Latin American countries when writing to my representatives. In the 1970s, 1980s, and 1990s, I shared my concerns about U.S. support of governments in Central and South America during the numerous civil wars in these countries. The members of Congress with whom I corresponded were concerned at that time with the spread of communism, and they did not appear to pay a lot of attention to my opinions. Nevertheless, I continued to write. Eventually others *did* listen, and I learned that it is indeed worthwhile to focus on one issue.

In April 1989 I was asked to join the staff of the Presbytery of New Covenant, a regional office of the Presbyterian Church, U.S.A., as the Associate General Presbyter for Justice and Compassion. What a title! I got to work on social issues on behalf of the Presbyterian Church in a regional governing body that included 112 congregations in 34 counties in Southeastern Texas. My work served to crystallize my relationships with Central American issues and my representatives in Washington, D.C. I traveled to Washington D.C. several times a year to work on social justice issues on behalf of the church. While there, I was able to develop good working relationships with the Congressional offices that represent the southern parts of the State of Texas.

Another area of responsibility I had at that time was to lead an annual trip to visit Christian communities in Central America. The Presbytery developed a partnership with the Center of Evangelical Pastoral Studies in Central America. Since the Center's work encompassed all Central American countries, we traveled to each of the countries, visiting with people and learning about the Center's ministries. On our trips to Central America we encountered a recurring theme: a few people lived very well while many families lived in poverty. Indeed these countries were divided between the people who had work, money and power and those who did not. During the civil wars that arose out of these inequalities, numerous peasants were killed in the countryside, and we learned about the churches' ministries within those communities.

On one of the trips to Central America, I had the opportunity to listen to a Roman Catholic priest in El Salvador. He described the situation in his country. El Salvador was then in the middle of a horrible civil war where many civilians and military personnel were being wounded or killed. The El Salvadoran Church also had its martyrs, such as Bishop Romero, who was killed while serving Holy Communion on March 24, 1980. Four nuns from the United States were killed in November of the same year. In 1989, six Jesuit priests and two women were murdered outside their homes. They had criticized the Salvadoran government. The priest's reports were confirmed by what we heard on the nightly news: stories of brutal atrocities that had occurred in El Salvador. When the priest from El Salvador became aware that I traveled to Washington each year to visit Congressional offices, and that I had good contacts with several members of Congress, he offered to provide me with information regarding the civil war. He would share his daily updates via fax on the civil war in his country. Our partnership was formed.

The El Salvadoran priest delivered newsworthy information almost immediately on my return home. I remember the first Monday I reported back to work in the United States. A fax arrived describing the deaths of some Salvadoran people. I did not keep these faxes, but I can paraphrase them in this way: "Today, the Salvadoran military entered village XYZ and killed so many people." The date was stated along with the time of day. This fax and each one that followed listed the name, age and sex of the individuals who were killed. Each fax put the blame for killing civilians squarely on the Salvadoran military personnel.

I was shocked when I received the first fax because its information was so fresh. So I shared the fax with my boss, the Executive General Presbyter of the Presbytery, who encouraged me to send the information to Washington. I translated the fax from Spanish to English, put the information on the Presbytery's stationary, and sent it to the office of my Congressional Representative, who at the time was Mr. Bill Archer. The fax was received in his office by the aide whose job included keeping up-to-date on this Central American issue. I asked this aide to relay the fax to the State Department in order to confirm that the skirmish between the Salvadoran military and the guerrillas or freedom fighters had actually taken place.

Later in the day, I received a confirmation from Mr. Archer's Office regarding my earlier fax. The response was something like this: "The State Department has confirmed that the events described in your fax are correct. But the military personnel have stated that the guerrillas started the skirmish and the military merely defended themselves." Messages like these went back and forth almost daily for about three months. Each fax I sent claimed that the military had started the skirmish, while the State Department's response through the Congressional Office was always that the guerrilla movement in El Salvador had started the battle.

I had written numerous letters to my Congressional Representatives in New Jersey, Illinois, New Mexico and Texas arguing against sending military aid to Central and South America. Now I had concrete evidence that the military in El Salvador were killing their own people. Each fax I sent to Washington was being confirmed as true. Each skirmish was occurring. I also received confirmation that military personnel in El Salvador were killing women and children. So I decided to change my tone to my Congressional Representative. Instead of asking my Representative to quit voting for military aid all the time, I decided to ask him to go 50-50 with me. Instead of voting for military aid 100% of the time, I asked him to find some way to not vote for such aid half the time.

The faxes continued to arrive with alarming and dependable regularity. Each one I forwarded blamed the military personnel in El Salvador. The Congressional Office's responses from Washington, D.C., based on information provided by the State Department, continued to state that the guerrilla movement was at fault. The

Representative's response to me was that war is war, and, yes, occasionally civilians die. He said there is no way he would change the way he voted because the majority of the constituents in his district in Texas thought stamping out communism was more important than objecting to military actions against civilians. Since I was in the minority, I decided I had to change my strategy once again and educate my fellow constituents.

Educating constituents who do not want to have anything to do with politics is a difficult task indeed. I started to attend each town hall meeting sponsored by Congressman Archer. I went to listen to the concerns of the people living in the district. I became disillusioned because my Congressman was right. There was a strong feeling in the district that communism needed to be stamped out in all parts of the world. But my church was asking that justice be done. How could we stand idle and let relatively few families in each Central American country have all the power, prosperity and economic benefits while using the military to protect their privileges as was happening in El Salvador? The more I listened to the voters in my Congressional District the more I realized the immense task I faced in changing minds and hearts.

Then I received what I came to call "the fax that broke the camel's back." It was eight pages long and contained over 200 names of people who had been killed. Many of them were women and children, and infants. Would this report speak to the hearts of my government contacts? As with the rest of the faxes, I translated it and sent it to Mr. Archer's office. The young aide in the office who was responsible for this issue called me as soon as he received this fax. I could tell there were tears in his eyes. It was obvious he was listening with his heart. I heard him crying as he repeated: "This can't be true. Tom, it can't be true." I asked him to do the same thing with this fax that he had done with the others. He said he already had sent the fax on to the State Department. He told me that the woman at the State Department who was in charge of El Salvador issues had asked how I received this information so quickly.

So I shared with the aide that I had a church connection. I told him that often the church goes to places in the Third World where our government workers cannot go. In Latin America, representatives of our government are sometimes sheltered from the big picture of how life really is in the countries where they are working. I explained that El Salvador's civil war was a struggle for freedom for all the people.

There was a rich class who controlled the government, businesses and the land. Then there were the poor who struggled to survive by eating whatever they could find in the dump. Guerrillas fought to provide some land and a place to call home for all those who lived in the dump. The ruling class on the other hand would not relinquish their status in the society. The Church was more in touch with those who lived in poverty than any representative of the United States Government could ever be.

The aide said, "Well, the woman in the State Department would like for you to send the faxes to her directly from now on, and she would like to discuss this issue with you further. May I give her your phone number so the two of you can discuss this issue directly with each other?" I assured him that would be okay, and that I would look forward to hearing from this woman.

My faxes were deemed reliable, and they demonstrated that the Salvadoran military, which our government's policy supported, was killing civilians. Five minutes after I finished speaking with the aide, the woman from the State Department called. She too had been listening with her heart. She expressed dismay at the fatalities itemized in the fax. She was curious how I was providing information that the U.S. embassy in El Salvador didn't have. I asked her if she had ever traveled to El Salvador. She said that she had not.

This did not surprise me. Several times during visits to El Salvador with groups of church people, I was taken to the U.S. Embassy for a visit. During those visits, I learned that the U.S. Embassy in El Salvador was the most expensive embassy that our nation had built anywhere in the world at that time. I was told the embassy cost something like $80 million dollars to build. It is a fortress. The outside wall measures a good 15 feet wide at the base. There is a massive security gate through which visitors must enter. The people who work in the embassy live within its walled compound. The embassy needed to be a fortress because the policies of our government were not popular with most people in El Salvador. But some of the defenses that keep danger out can also keep ideas and information out. I cannot count the number of times I heard from the Salvadoran people I visited: "You need not be afraid of us. We don't like your government. We like you as a people, but your policies need to change!" This was news to the woman at the State Department. She requested that I send the faxes directly to her without translating them first, because they had Spanish-speaking people in the State Department.

From then on I forwarded the casualty lists from the Salvadoran priest directly to the State Department.

Before ending my conversation with the woman from the State Department, I asked that our government urged the El Salvadoran government to seek peace with the FMLN (Farabundo Marti National Liberation) and the FDR (Revolutionary Democracy Front), their opponents in the civil war. Since 1931, the military had governed El Salvador. They had used military force to attempt to bring peace, but I argued the evidence of the killing of innocent civilians was a reason to try harder for a true peaceful solution to the civil war.

Not long after my conversation with the woman at the State Department, I read in my local newspaper that the United States Government had requested the Salvadoran government to seek a peaceful solution to their war with the guerrilla movement. Six to nine months after "the fax that broke the camel's back," the newspapers reported that our government was encouraging the guerrillas and the government officials in El Salvador to develop a roadmap for peace. On January 16, 1992, Peace Accords were signed! Victory at last! Since then, it has not been an easy transition for the military and the guerrillas or freedom fighters to move toward peace. However, I am convinced that there never would have been a chance for peace if people along the way had not listened with their hearts and then, in turn, thought of ways in which they could speak to the hearts of others with the power to make necessary changes in government policy. To listen with the heart implies a willingness to work things through. My personal efforts on this war front started when I was a young student in New Jersey. Thirty years later, peace became a reality. Governments never work rapidly. They have to take time to make sure that the solutions they seek are the best ones for their citizens. I'm grateful the U.S. government was willing to reconsider its policies and make changes.

Rev. Tomás Spath

True civility requires knowing yourself and then being willing to forge relationships with others through listening, with our strength, mind and heart. Listening with our hearts may be the riskiest of all behaviors needed to foster civility. Truly listening with our hearts open to the reality of what we are hearing opens us to the risk of change, always a scary proposition. When we are able to listen to one another with all of our being, however, civility happens.

Rule # 8: Trust, Trust, Trust

"Trust your hopes, not your fears."
David Mahoney

"There is no more perfect endowment in man than political virtue."
Author Unknown (inscribed on the wall of Houston City Hall foyer)

Trust is a willingness to rely on the integrity of another person. It is earned over time, and lost in a heart beat. When we trust others, we rely on their honesty. We expect and hope that their actions will be in accordance with the persons they represent themselves to be in their interactions with others. One side of the coin of trust is risk, the risk that our trust may be unjustified or abused. The other side of that coin, however, is hope and a willingness to believe that good people indeed exist and that they will do what they have promised.

The legal tender of the United States, the money we use to buy things, says "In God We Trust." Even for those of deep faith, however, trusting in God can seem risky at times. How then can one risk trusting mere mortals, including politicians, to do what they promise and to act in accordance with their public personae, the persons whom they represent themselves to be? Many people believe that the things that matter most to politicians are power, prestige, money, and of course reelection. However, this perceived reality is not always the case. For what enables our government to function is the willingness of our elected officials to trust each other. Without that basic foundation, the difficult compromises necessary to govern become impossible. Therefore, especially in Washington, D.C., trust is the coin of the realm. And with trust comes civility, for the two go hand-in-hand, building on one another.

For those with little practical experience in the workings of representative government, stating the importance of trust in Washington, D.C. may sound absurd, especially to constituents who feel their trust has been betrayed on many occasions. For example, too many have observed a representative whom they helped elect promise one thing during the campaign, but do something entirely different once elected. Or insist they are telling the truth, but then later events demonstrate a falsehood. Two brief examples are when former Republican President George Bush Sr., looking directly into a TV camera proclaimed in a debate before the election, "Read my lips, no new taxes." Promptly thereafter, upon his election to the Presidency, he felt a need to raise taxes. The public also felt betrayed when former Democratic President Bill Clinton promised our country that he "did not have sexual relations with that woman" referring to a young intern in the White House, but learned later that was not true. Too often the public perception is that politicians are at the bottom of the list of people who can be trusted. Unfortunately, enough examples of poor public leadership exist to make it difficult at times for citizens to perceive integrity, and the trust earned by that integrity, in political campaigns and the subsequent maneuvering that a democratic form of government requires.

But the reality for elected officials in Washington, D.C., and in our state and local governments as well, is that there is no surer way to gain lasting friends and influence than by proving themselves worthy of trust. And there is no surer way to lose influence and the ability to function than to betray someone who has trusted them to work for the well being of their constituents. One of the most painful aspects of broken trust is that once broken, it is difficult, if not impossible, to regain. Those who have experienced broken trust in their personal lives will understand why the ability to trust someone is invaluable. They will also understand the all too human temptation to be less than civil to those who have abused our trust. We are blessed if we are among that small group without stories to tell of trust broken. More than likely each of us has a visceral understanding of how it feels to be betrayed by someone we trusted. Broken trust is not something any of us would willingly court.

There is also a darker side to "trusting" others to act in accord with their public personae. Some develop a well deserved negative reputation based on their past actions. Others learn to "trust" that such people will indeed act in accordance with their past behavior--that is they will live *down* to their reputations. Some members of Congress can always be trusted to vote the party position. Some can always be trusted to speak on an issue and to be in front of the cameras. Some can be trusted to refuse both to support their colleagues and to work with representatives with different political views. And, unfortunately, some can be trusted to resort to politics at its dirtiest level, consistently failing to maintain civility in their interactions with their colleagues.

Constituents earn reputations as well. Some are known as people committed to the democratic process, as individuals who can be trusted to tirelessly volunteer for campaigns, attend town hall meetings, write letters, and be active in their communities. Not all constituents can be trusted to behave responsibly however. Some have come to be known as people willing to buy votes, as angry voters who yell and badger, but will not listen, or as apathetic citizens unwilling to educate themselves on issues or to listen to another side of an issue. Some can be trusted to do nothing but complain without ever trying to be part of a constructive solution.

A reputation earned for either good behavior or destructive actions shadows individuals for a long time. An individual's reputation as a person who can or cannot be trusted can make dialogue and working with that person either easier or more difficult. Our reputations impact our ability to engage in civil interactions, both in everyday life and in the political arena. Most, if not all, of us operate our daily lives based upon trust or lack thereof. We trust that the police and firefighters will come and protect us when we call. We trust our personal physicians to act in our best interests. We trust that the mechanic we have patronized for years will repair our car when we request service. We trust that our pastor will be there in our time of need. When our trust of another proves ill-founded, we act with circumspection in any future interactions with that person. Politicians too learn who can and who cannot be trusted from their interactions with fellow politicians and constituents.

Trust in Action

The following story from Cassandra Dahnke and Tomás Spath demonstrates how trust functions in practice in Washington, D.C.

We have found in our experiences working with the Institute for Civility in Government that trust has been critical to our accomplishments. One of the Institute's primary activities is scheduling forums at which students can interact with members of Congress. While we are always glad to have the participation of members of Congress in Congressional Student Forums, we naturally tend to gravitate toward those whom we have learned from past experience can be trusted to model civility, and who keep partisanship to a minimum when they interact with the students and another member of Congress with different political views. Of necessity we think very carefully before extending an invitation to those who have a reputation for lambasting others. Like most people, we have our own stories of trust broken. However, telling those stories would put us in the position of further eroding trust already compromised. Fortunately, it is easier and more productive to find examples of those who can be trusted. Such examples have taught us how trust helps to move the process of governing forward while encouraging civility in that process.

Often when we are in Washington, D. C. on behalf of the Institute, one Congressional office will refer us to another. Even though we have had no prior contact with the office to which we are referred, that office will make time to see us, even if it is a last minute request. They make the time to talk with us based on the strength of a referral from a colleague whom they trust. We are not high profile people, but we have established relationships based on trust with Congressional staff members with whom we have become acquainted. Congressional offices are also willing to see us without knowing us because of the trusting relationships that have been established between different Congressional offices. Trust is the coin of the realm in Washington, D.C.

In 2000, Congressman Nick Lampson initiated a conversation between The Faith and Politics Institute and the Institute for Civility in Government. We had never heard of The Faith and Politics Institute, a non-profit organization that "works to encourage spiritual growth and conscience in public life, [that] is interfaith and non-partisan." Among its many activities are forums held for members of Congress at which a wide array of guest speakers are presented. The Faith and Politics Institute had never heard of the Institute for Civility in Government, which at that time was only two years old. We had just begun our journey. Congressman Lampson, however, was familiar with both organizations, and he saw a connection. Because both organizations knew Nick Lampson, The Faith and Politics Institute trusted his judgment when he suggested us as guest speakers for one of their Congressional forums, and we trusted his recommendation that we work with another institute with which we were unfamiliar.

A conversation between the two organizations began. As a result, The Faith and Politics Institute agreed to host a forum for members of Congress at which we would be the featured speakers. They were willing to do this even though they did not know us, had never met us, and were not familiar with our work, because they knew and trusted Nick Lampson. They accepted some risk in issuing their invitation for us to speak at one of their forums. The Faith and Politics Institute has held many successful events through its years on Capitol Hill. But even one unsuccessful event could blemish an otherwise pristine history of accomplishment. They did not know at the time how much interest there would be in the issue of civility, and they did not know if we would be good speakers. They also did not know if anyone would come to hear us speak.

We first met the folks at the Faith and Politics Institute the morning of the event. They were very gracious in receiving us, and at the same time somewhat intrigued. The number of R.S.V.P.'s they had received from members of Congress suggested the topic of civility was garnering more interest than they had anticipated. Our particular forum was "hosted" by Representatives Bill Archer, Ken Bentsen, Kevin Brady, Amos Houghton, Nick Lampson, and John Lewis. That fact that this forum was hosted by so many Congressmen who were well known, well respected, and quite powerful no doubt had quite a bit to do with the attention we received.

The Tuesday morning in June that we were scheduled to speak was a very busy one in Congress. Many members were intensely involved in what are called "mark-ups," the process in which a committee responsible for reviewing or drafting a piece of legislation does its final work on the proposed law before it goes to the House floor for a vote. We knew those committee meetings were where many members of Congress needed to be. As we arrived in the room in the Capitol where we were to speak and waited for the meeting to begin, we took the opportunity to soak up the history, beauty, and power of the Capitol, the symbol of our democracy. And we wondered if anyone would show up.

Sixteen members came to the forum at which we spoke. That was an extraordinary number of participants under the circumstances. Even more impressive, however, was the fact that they stayed for a full hour, actively participated and asked questions, and did not want to leave. Our meeting ended only when we, and the representatives with whom we were still speaking, were firmly ushered out of the room by the workers who had to prepare it for the next event.

From this single forum at which we spoke many wonderful working relationships were initiated between the Institute for Civility in Government and members of Congress who had not previously been involved with the Institute. We were able to schedule Congressional Student Forums that would otherwise never have happened. But it all began based on a simple recommendation to two organizations that had never heard of each other, but knew they could trust Representative Nick Lampson.

The power of trust to build relationships and enhance civility cannot be overstated. Relationships built on trust make civil dialogue on difficult issues easier. Civil dialogue with those we trust is possible even when we must disagree on issues of importance.

Rule # 9: One is Powerful

"Remember that you are needed. There is at least one important work to be done that will not be done unless you do it."
- Charles Allen

"You must be the change you wish to see in the world." -
Mohandas Ghandi

Many of us feel powerless to make changes in our lives or in the lives of others. Too often we feel even less able to influence the climate of our national government and our society. However, we need only look at the close vote in two national elections in the beginning of the 21st century to realize that individual actions really do make a difference in our democracy. We have the unique opportunity in our country to be heard, to organize, and to make our feelings known-- rights not enjoyed by many others on the planet.

For many years, Cassandra Dahnke and Tomás Spath have been making annual trips to Washington, D.C. to meet with members of Congress on behalf of the Institute. Initially, they met with members of Congress who knew them from their earlier work leading annual legislative conferences to Washington D.C. with members of the Presbyterian church. Meetings with these members of Congress were easy to arrange because relaionships had already been established.Trust and understanding had been built over time, and the members with whom they arranged meetings knew Cassandra and Tomás, and had become familiar with the work and concerns of the Institute.

As the Institute's work has spread through the years to encompass a larger geographic area, however, Cassandra and Tomás have been blessed with opportunities to seek meetings with members of Congress whom they have never met, people who are not familiar with the Institute or its work. Getting an appointment with a member of Congress can be a challenge when you are an unknown entity, particularly if you are not a constituent from that member's Congressional district.

Members of Congress are in Washington, D.C. to represent the people who live in their districts, so they are sensitive to constituent concerns. Cassandra and Tomás have learned that a phone call or letter from even a single member of the Institute who lives in a Congressional member's District usually creates the opportunity for a meeting with the member of Congress or their staff. Some may view this process with cynicism and question the sincerity of Congressional representatives or their staff. But the process in fact demonstrates the difference a single voice can make. Often one phone call makes it possible for the Institute's concerns to be heard. Each of us has more power to affect our political climate than we may realize, especially when we engage in the process with civility.

PROOF THAT ONE IS POWERFUL

The following story told from the perspectives of Cassandra Dahnke and Donna Bowling demonstrates the power of a single Institute member to help the Institute accomplish its work.

For many years, as Tomás Spath and I have gone to Washington, D.C. to meet with members of Congress and their staff, we have been learning how to navigate the terrain on Capitol Hill. We know our way around the Senate and House Office buildings, and we understand such mysteries as the Byzantine systems of phone numbers and numbering of the Congressional offices. Prior to the September 11, 2001 terror attacks on New York and Washington, we knew the basement of the Capitol almost as well as anyone. Now only those who are escorted may go there. We even knew where the closet was where the extra water pitchers were kept and who had the key! We know the sound of heels clacking on the marble floors and the beauty of chandeliers, ornate staircases, and impressive statues of the great statesmen in our country's past. We know where some of the more obscure elevators and stairways are located. We know how to dress, who to call, where to go, and how to speak in the strange environment of our federal government.

As a result of our work, we now know quite a few members of Congress and have developed lasting relationships with many staff members. We have learned many, if not all, of the rules for working effectively in Washington, D.C. We work well with people from both sides of the political aisle, i.e. people of both major political parties. We have received letters from members of Congress commending our skills, praising our efforts and urging us forward in our work for the Institute.

Nonetheless, we cannot schedule an appointment with anyone we want whenever we want it. Congressional offices receive thousands of letters and hundreds of requests for meetings every year. It is extremely difficult for any Congressional office to honor every single request that is made, even when using every person available on staff. Our elected representatives must make choices when scheduling meetings in order to have enough time to perform their job of representing all of their constituents.

Many offices choose to meet only with constituents from the district or state they represent. The Institute is based in Houston, Texas, because that is where its co-founders live, and where we began our work for civility. Initially when we approach a Congressional office outside the bounds of the Houston area, we may receive a polite refusal when we request to meet with a Representative or Senator. We understand that this is nothing personal. It is simply a function of how a particular office determines with whom they will meet.

When we encounter such a refusal, we do our best to explain why we are approaching that particular office, and why we believe that office should be interested in meeting with us as representatives of the Institute. Frequently we explain we want a meeting with the Representative or Senator because there are members of the Institute who live within the Congressional district or state the member of Congress represents. Often that is the only explanation we need in order to secure a meeting, but not always. Occasionally there are offices that are still unwilling to arrange a meeting with us. That is when we depend on the strength of the voices of our members. That is when we are reminded that one is powerful.

On more than one occasion we have phoned members of the Institute who live in a specific Congressional district and asked them to call or write their Congressional office, requesting that they meet with us. Each time the members have been happy to comply, and each time the results have been dramatic. The doors of access to members of Congress and their staffs have gone from closed to wide open--sometimes in a matter of minutes! Why? Because Congress counts each single voice it hears as being representative of hundreds of others. So every voice our representatives hear carries the weight of many more. Suddenly a Congressional office will work diligently to arrange a meeting with us. Again, this is nothing false or personal. The Washington reality is simply that messages spoken by a single voice, when that person is a constituent are heard in a different way and with more urgency.

Rev. Cassandra Dahnke

MORE PROOF ONE IS POWERFUL

Cassandra and Tomás wanted to arrange a Congressional Student Forum in Central Texas and hoped to involve Representative Chet Edwards in that process. Representative Edwards was my Congressional Representative prior to the redistricting that took place in 2004. He is an intelligent, dedicated individual who is held in high regard by many of those, like me, whom he has represented for many years. As is the case with other Congressional Representatives, he cannot routinely meet with each and every organization or individual that contacts his office, no matter how well meaning.

Representative Edwards was a member of Congress with whom Cassandra Dahnke and Tomás Spath had not yet worked. Because I lived in his district, Cassandra asked me to contact his office and request that someone from his office meet with Cassandra and Tomás while they were in Washington, D.C. for their annual trip. I admit that I was skeptical a contact from me would accomplish what they needed, although I have a high regard for Representative Edwards and have corresponded with his office a number of times.

However, because of Cassandra's request I contacted Representative Edwards' local office. I asked how to fax a letter to his Washington, D.C. office, where he was at the time as Congress was in session. The local office promptly provided me with the fax number. I sent a letter describing the Institute and requesting that Representative Edwards take time to meet with Cassandra and Tomás. Cassandra told me that after my letter arrived, they received a prompt call back and were able to schedule a meeting with Rep. Edwards and a member of his staff. I was reminded by this experience that elected officials really do listen. I learned that one person can have a powerful impact. I have become convinced that Cassandra and Tomás are correct: One voice is powerful.

Donna Bowling

When we are firm in our own beliefs and our reasons for holding those beliefs, a stance enhanced by respectful interaction with others of differing beliefs, we are empowered to speak up on behalf of issues of importance, including our desire for civility. By exercising our individual power and raising our voice in a civil fashion, we enrich our community dialogue and demonstrate civility for others, making it easier for them to respond in kind. Throughout history ordinary individuals have changed the world through their actions. One voice speaking up on issues of importance in a civil fashion has great power.

Rule #10: Numbers Count

"Never doubt that a small group of thoughtful, committed citizens can change the world; indeed it is the only thing that ever has."
- Margaret Mead

"What counts is that there is a fledgling group struggling to take the return of civility one step at a time."
- Jane Ely, editorial columnist for the <u>Houston Chronicle,</u> writing about the Institute for Civility in Government.

It is unfortunate that we must organize to promote civility, but the political climate is such that organizing those who value civility to increase the impact of their voices is necessary. The truth is that history demonstrates that within the human community, we do not automatically or necessarily receive what is right, fair, or desirable. What we may receive, however, are those things for which we are willing to organize and work together.

Senior politicians, who were active in the governing process years ago, remember that process as one characterized by vigorous debate, followed by laughter and camaraderie when the day's work was done. People who could not agree politically about much except that democracy was valuable--meant to be appreciated, cultivated, and protected--nonetheless shared friendship and respect. Today too many people seem willing to relegate the civility inherent in those earlier dynamics to the dustbin of fond memories from yesteryear, back in the good old days.

Civility is not an anachronism, however, as the Institute's members demonstrate by joining. The existence of the Institute demonstrates that civility is an important priority and that the way we make decisions is often as important as the decisions that result and the positions that we take. One voice can have a powerful effect, but more voices joined together can have an even *greater* impact. The issues, positions, and candidates that receive the most attention from the media, the public and our elected officials are often the ones that have the most popular support. For groups like the Institute, this means the more members an organization has, the greater the possibility of having an impact.

Institute membership demonstrates belief in civility as a tangible goal. While individual members have their opinions and take positions on issues, the Institute does not. Nor does it support or oppose anyone running for office. What the Institute does through its members is build a presence for civility within the community dynamic. Individually a person who values civility might be discouraged and inclined to give up the effort. Together with other members organized into the Institute, however, people find the encouragement and the support necessary to continue seeking and fostering civility for everyone. There was a reason Jesus sent the disciples out in twos! Martin Luther King, Jr. and the civil rights movement had an impact because of the numbers of people who were willing to participate. Cesar Chavez and the farm workers also received attention because of the numbers involved with their activities. In the first decade of the 21st century, massive demonstrations by immigrants in the U.S. responding to legislation proposed in Congress have focused attention on the need for comprehensive reform of U.S. immigration laws. Numbers count.

The more people who are involved in the Institute, the stronger its influence becomes. Numbers count in many ways. Obviously, numbers of votes and the numbers of people holding an opinion matter. Through our individual and collective votes we determine who will be elected. Through our individual and collective voices, we also inform those in power about issues and positions that we consider important. Each person who joins the Institute increases the likelihood of media coverage in their local community concerning civility. Each provides additional opportunities to catch the attention of elected officials. Each member strengthens the presence of the Institute and thereby improves the tone of community life. Growth in Institute membership has resulted in the Institute's greater ability to facilitate public dialogue among people who think differently, to teach respect and to increase civility in the governing process.

Rep. Bill Archer's Town Hall Meeting

The following story from Cassandra Dahnke demonstrates the powerful effect of many people responding in concert.

For many years I have tried to attend as many town hall and community meetings as I can. These are meetings that Congressional Representatives schedule back home in their districts as a way to meet with their constituents. I do not go to the meetings to speak, but rather to listen to what is being said. My goal is to find out what the Representatives are hearing from concerned citizens and to listen to the tone of the meetings. Because I used to be in Representative Bill Archer's district, I went to many of his meetings. Some of these meetings were quite small, but most drew between 200 and 500 participants.

In the early spring after the Republican Party had just won the majority in Congress in the fall of 1994, I attended one of Representative Bill Archer's town hall meetings that was extremely well attended. Representative Archer had just become the new chair of the House Ways and Means committee, an important position. At one point fairly early in the meeting, a woman stood up and Representative Archer called on her. She proceeded to loudly and ferociously berate him because a few weeks earlier he had met with then President Clinton regarding some budget issues. This meeting had received quite a bit of publicity across the country as Representative Archer had gone to meet with the President alone, on his own initiative and not as a part of the Republican House Leadership's strategy. I am not even sure the House leadership knew about the meeting before it took place.

The woman angrily complained to Representative Archer, "Don't you know that the Republicans have FINALLY won the majority after all these years?" She demanded to know how he had dared to go and talk to the president--a DEMOCRAT! She insisted that now was the chance Republicans had been waiting for to do what THEY wanted to do regarding national policy. Representative Archer literally could not get a word in edgewise as this woman continued to scold him for nearly five minutes. Finally, she quit talking and he was able to respond to her specific concerns. Rather than responding to what those present perceived as a personal attack on him and his judgment, he calmly assured her he was aware of the Republican majority. He then focused on the budget issues at hand that all parties needed to address. His response, which addressed the issues rather than challenging the woman for the uncivil way in which she presented her concerns, was appropriate under the circumstances. Had Representative Archer responded by directly challenging her behavior, he would have distracted attention from the legislative issue being discussed; possibly been seen as responding by way of a personal attack—uncivil behavior of a different sort; and perhaps escalated the argument rather than fostering further dialogue. His approach was to focus on issues, not personalities. By responding calmly and not being drawn into a shouting match or name calling, he demonstrated civility by his example.

Shortly after this exchange, Rep. Archer called on another woman, and she stood up near the front of the room. Although I was sitting near the back, I could see that the second woman was shaking.

Perhaps she was shaking because she was nervous, but I think it is far more likely that she was so angry she was simply trembling with indignation. She said, "Excuse me. I was under the impression this was a town hall meeting and not a Republican rally. I came here to discuss issues. I am a Democrat. That woman (pointing to the woman who had berated Representative Archer's judgment earlier) has just called me every name in the book, and I am highly offended." She sat down. Representative Archer responded, thanking the woman for her presence. He emphasized that this was indeed intended as a town hall meeting at which everyone was welcome to speak and he welcomed her input. He then moved on to others who had questions. After a short while, the second woman stood up and left the meeting, perhaps too upset to stay. As she left, several people in the crowd broke out in loud applause and catcalls. They yelled "Good riddance!" and "Let the door hit you on the way out!" and other similar ugly remarks.

I sat quietly for another 30 to 45 minutes through the remainder of the meeting. Near the end I raised my hand, and Representative Archer called on me. I stood up and said, "Bill, you know me, and you know I come to a lot of your town hall meetings to listen to what folks have to say. I've never said anything, but I cannot let this one go by. I want you to know that for every person who is angry at you for having spoken with the President about the budget, I believe many more of us are simply thankful that you are focusing on the problem and are working with others to try and get something done." To my surprise, as I sat back down, the audience burst into loud and sustained applause.

Prior to my comments and the response of those attending the meeting, everyone in that room, including Representative Archer, would probably have left the meeting with the impression that divisive, ugly, and rude behavior is perfectly acceptable, and that those who had displayed it were probably in the majority. After all, the actions of those half dozen people who had loudly and rudely celebrated the departure of the second woman who spoke had seemingly gone unchallenged. How was anyone to know these individuals did not speak for the majority of those present? However, when I spoke up, others who shared my view expressed their feelings with their applause. Everyone came away with a very different understanding-- a belief that the majority of those present DID want to cooperate and work through problems, and DIDN'T want to be rude or antagonistic. Others at the meeting who agreed with me left knowing many who were there valued civility and constructive action--a very different feeling than they would have had if no one had responded when I spoke up. The response from many to my comments created a powerful impression. Numbers count!

Rev. Cassandra Dahnke

Knowing our own beliefs is important. So is listening with respect to the beliefs of others. When individual voices speak with civility in concert with many other such voices, the effect is powerful indeed.

PART 3: THE CHALLENGE

GO FOR IT!

*"It is not because things are difficult that we do not dare;
it is because we do not dare that they are difficult."*
- Seneca, Stoic philosopher and writer of mid-1ˢᵗ century Rome

*"Those who say something cannot be done should get out
of the way of the people who are doing it."*
- Author Unknown

It is not difficult today to find people who share a concern about the lack of civility in our society in general, and our public discourse in particular. What is difficult is to find people who believe they can do anything about the degree of civility in our political processes beyond remaining civil themselves. To say that people are apathetic and cynical about their ability to affect how our political process works addresses only one part of the problem. Many who sit on the sidelines profess to care deeply about our government, our nation, and the lives of its people. Yet they feel powerless to bring about positive change and enhance civility in our political interactions.

We've heard it said there are two kinds of people in society-- those who get things done and those who don't. Sitting idly by and watching the world go around will not help us bring more civility to the governing process. We need active citizens. We need citizens who will be not only active members of a particular nation, but also ones who will take an active part in making our local communities and our world a better place. We need all of us.

Recent books, such as <u>Bowling Alone</u> by Robert Putnam and <u>Hope Unraveled</u> by Richard Harwood, have pointed toward a trend of increasing isolation among individuals within the United States today. We no longer volunteer as much as we have in the past. Rather than going out and actively bringing about more civil interactions in our communities, we are withdrawing into small circles peopled with others who think like us. We gather with only a few close friends and choose to stay there while assuming others will take care of societal concerns. That might be okay if just a few of us were taking this approach to life. The problem is that more and more of the others we assume are taking care of things are withdrawing as well.

A transformation needs to take place, and it must start with us. If we the people of the United States choose to be more civil, we can change our nation and ultimately have an impact on the rest of the world. But if we choose instead to sit on the sidelines, interacting with only a chosen few, then the polarization occurring in our public square will likely continue to grow.

Following the rules presented in the previous chapters builds civility. The stories illustrating the rules demonstrate that civility can be fostered, even in our political processes. But before civility can flourish, it must first be cultivated, and that requires action by each of us. We each bear responsibility for fostering civility within our own relationships. Leading by example is essential. Being civil to others makes it easier for them to be civil to us. As the old saying goes, "What goes around comes around."

But beyond that, what can we do? The Institute was founded as a practical means of addressing this question. The Institute fosters civil governance by facilitating dialogue, teaching respect and building civility. The Institute does this by providing education. Through speaking engagements, workshops, seminars, and Congressional Student Forums, the Institute teaches people about civility and its importance. Our civility training gives tips on how to be civil and conducts exercises on listening and communicating well. The Institute also provides training for those who want to maintain civil discourse while being effective advocates for particular issues. This training teaches individuals to advocate while focusing on the importance relationship plays in successfully furthering a cause. Role-playing is used to help people practice what they learn.

Perhaps the greatest educational tool the Institute offers are the Congressional Student Forums it sponsors. These forums bring together two members of Congress, one Democrat and one Republican, to model civil discourse for high school and college students. The members of Congress who appear at these events speak respectfully to one another at these events while at the same time being honest about differences of opinion. The forums are not debates, but rather collegial dialogues. Though debates have their place and can be extremely instructive, they also set individuals and groups in opposition to one another, and do little to foster genuine dialogue. Debates are structured so that there is always a winner and a loser.

The Institute's Congressional Student Forums are presented at no charge and are held on college and university campuses. They offer students the opportunity to meet with U.S. Congressional Representatives in an atmosphere quite different from the rough and tumble of an election campaign. The students set the agenda. They are invited to pose questions to the members of Congress and to enter into dialogue with them on issues of the students' choosing. The emphasis is not on partisan politics, not on elections, not on who wins and loses, but on the process of talking with one another. For many of these students, this is their first personal experience in civic life. We believe the empowerment they receive and the civility that is practiced by all present sets an important precedent for their future civic involvement.

Offering educational experiences, however, as important as it is, is only one part of the Institute's approach to developing greater civility in the public sector. The other component of the Institute's efforts to develop civility is membership in the Institute: individuals who create a presence, a voice, for civility in the community dynamic. As discussed in the chapter on Rule #9, it is our membership that provides the impetus, clout, and resources that make it possible for education to take place, whether one on one, in a workshop, or in an auditorium full of hundreds of people. The Institute's members open doors, provide credibility and extend its influence and voice across communities and the nation to make a difference.

To those who have continued reading this far, who believe that civility is important, who long for significant dialogue instead of sound-bites or campaign speeches, who advocate for important issues, who wish to be positive role-models for generations to come, and who seek to safe-guard democracy at all levels of government, we issue an invitation. Please join us in the Institute! We cannot do all of this as well, as thoroughly, or in your community without you! Join us not only in putting the rules for civility into practice in your life and your community, but also by becoming a member of the Institute to increase its presence and spread its benefits into new locations.

Our actions can encourage civility in our communities. For seven years, Cassandra Dahnke and Tomás Spath led legislative conferences, which they developed, to Washington, D.C. for members of the Presbyterian Church (U.S.A.) from southeast Texas. These conferences were called The Church in Washington, and it was out of the experiences shared through this program that the seeds of the

Institute were sown. Those conferences and the Institute have had profound effects on those who have been involved. Participants have learned the mechanics of our democracy. They have learned how to identify issues of importance to them and how to become informed about these issues. They have practiced respectfully debating competing viewpoints and achieving consensus. Group members have learned how to approach government officials to offer their convictions and constructive suggestions.

Are you still uncertain? Does it still sound impossible, far-fetched? Read the remainder of Part 3 for stories of some of the individuals who have accepted the challenge and become involved with the Institute and who, on their own, have put the rules for civility into practice. They have found the rules to be true and powerful, and their lives and communities have been changed as a result. Their stories demonstrate that the rules for fostering civility work both locally and nationally.

SUCCESS STORIES OF INDIVIDUALS INVOLVED WHO HAVE ACCEPTED THE CHALLENGE: PROOF CIVILITY WORKS!

The success stories that follow come primarily out of the Church in Washington program, which provided the seeds for the Institute. This program was sponsored by the Presbytery of New Covenant, one of 153 regional governing bodies of the Presbyterian Church (USA). The co-founders of the Institute were employed by this governing group and led groups to Washington, D.C. for legislative conferences as a part of their responsibilities for the social justice programs of the Presbytery. Participants in this program hailed from one of the 112 congregations that form the Presbytery of New Covenant. They were mainly Presbyterian, though others also participated. The purpose of the program was to encourage each participant to establish a good working relationship with their elected officials so they could work together on issues of concern. Civility was the key to establishing such a working relationship.

Before the conference participants left for Washington, D.C., they had several orientation meetings. The first meeting introduced the participants to each other, provided an overview of the trip and group building exercises. Everyone present learned why each participant was participating and what they hoped to gain from the trip. Background materials were given to participants for further reading. In the second orientation meeting, participants made a list of issues they wanted to discuss with their representatives in Washington, D.C. From that list, the group chose eight to ten specific issues. Based on the issues chosen, Cassandra and Tomás then scheduled briefings to be held during the conference in Washington. The briefings were by various groups with expertise on the issues chosen. Representatives from those organizations met with conference participants to share information and their perspectives. Cassandra and Tomás also provided each participant with the church's position on each issue as well as any relevant media articles. The third orientation meeting was used to continue to build relationships between the participants, to practice communication skills, and to review basic information designed to insure a successful experience in Washington, D.C.

After they had attended the briefings in Washington, D.C., participants divided into smaller groups based on their personal interests. These smaller groups were responsible for drafting the entire group's position on their assigned issue. When the position draft was later presented to all the participants, further work was done by the group as a whole until a statement was created that all present agreed upon. This process for reaching consensus required each participant to open their mind and heart to issues and thought patterns that were very different from their own. From time to time, participants had to be reminded of the conference purpose: to build relationships between ourselves as individuals and our elected officials.

Reaching consensus required everyone involved to learn the art of compromise. To create a statement that everyone could support, participants had to work hard at understanding others' points of view. There were moments when Cassandra and Tomás had to work with some individuals separately so they could hear what someone had said during a meeting, or so they could better articulate their own thoughts. As leaders of the conference, however, they were committed to the idea that people who come together to make a decision on something need to hear the perspectives of all involved in making that decision in order to begin finding common ground.

The participants in these legislative conferences never agreed on everything, and that was to be expected. Cassandra and Tomás always encouraged participants to remain true to their own convictions. If they gave up their position simply to get along with the group, then the final position statement would lack integrity, and there was a risk those who failed to stick with their convictions might go home angry, or disappointed and believing they had not been heard.

On the other hand, conference participants were always surprised by how much they could agree upon. They struggled, and reached consensus regarding specific pieces of legislation, not just general concepts. As a result, they came away with a new appreciation for the challenges facing members of Congress as they deal with many competing needs and demands, complex issues and limited resources.

So read the stories of those who participated in this program. Learn how they had to listen, be patient, respectfully express their position and work hard at dealing with participants who had a different point of view. These people were some of the first to join the Institute. They had seen for themselves the importance of participating in the governing process, the potential it holds for our society, and the essential role civility plays in working well together to address complex and difficult issues. Then envision the possibilities for your own such work in your community. Working together, community by community, we can achieve wonders and begin to transform the world in which we live. Staying at home and building strong relationships with only a few like-minded individuals may be easier and safer, but working together will allow us to create a better community for us all.

THE CO-FOUNDERS OF THE INSTITUTE

Cassandra Dahnke and Tomás Spath first met when Cassandra was hired by New Covenant Presbytery as a hunger action enabler. Tomás, as the Associate General Presbyter and Associate for Justice and Compassion, was her supervisor. Their job responsibilities required both of them to provide advice, counsel and resources to Houston area Presbyterian churches on social justice issues. Each brought a measure of education, practical experience, faith and compassion to their tasks. Perhaps that is why they were both so surprised when they suddenly discovered they came at many of the social justice issues they worked on from opposite political perspectives.

Cassandra and Tomás had just attended a meeting in downtown Houston on a hot afternoon, when they were walking back to the car along a broken sidewalk. Despite the heat, bits of bright green grass grew up through the sidewalk gaps, brushing the bottom of their shoes as they walked, talking and processing all they had just heard regarding the problems of Houston's poor and homeless population. While the views presented at the meeting had differed, those present had agreed that more needed to be done to address the needs of this group of vulnerable people.

The question Tomás and Cassandra were discussing was exactly what should and could be done and by whom? One thought that the poor needed more just treatment by government officials and that government programs were needed, while the other thought community organizations and individuals needed to get more involved in finding creative programs and fostering personal responsibility. They came to a complete stop as they realized their different philosophies were reflected not only in this particular issue, but in their voting histories. One was a Democrat, the other a Republican. They had discovered they were two people of faith with very different ideas about how to approach this problem. This is not an unusual occurrence among people of faith. What was unusual was their willingness to trust the relationship they had begun to establish and to work through their conflicts as they continued to approach tough issues from different perspectives while doing their jobs.

Their jobs as social justice advocates required them to discuss political issues with each other, whether they wanted to or not. When they found out they voted differently, they decided perhaps that fact would be of use to the growth of their program. They were forced to work intentionally through their differences. Even though they were both interested in the same social justice issues, they had very different ideas about how government should approach those issues. And even though they agreed on the applicable scriptures, they differed regarding how the church should apply those scriptures to the issues they discussed. Of course they also had very different ideas about how the government should be part of the solution to the social justice issues with which they worked.

They have continued to work through their differences about tough issues on a regular basis because they share a commitment to civility and a mutual respect for each other. Cassandra and Tomás have found ways to mediate their differences and seek win/win solutions for the issues they face. As they work towards common goals, they become committed to achieving them together. A part of that commitment is their willingness to listen to each other and try to understand how another person they respect can have such a different understanding of the issue in question. But they also maintain their own convictions and an understanding of why they hold them.

Cassandra and Tomás still approach most decisions and many issues from very different points of view, but both admit that over the years of working together they have influenced each other so their views of the world, their individual frames of reference, have moved closer together. However, even though each has had an effect on the other, neither has caved in simply to achieve consensus. Cassandra is no longer as sure about some things as she once was. Because she respects Tomás, she has been forced to reexamine her own beliefs when his are so very different, and vice versa. Tomás learned that her different approach to the elected officials and staff persons with whom they interacted on social justice issues was very effective-- perhaps more effective than his pure business-like approach as a seasoned advocate. He watched as Cassandra related to these people as individuals first – people with worries and cares and joys and loved ones just like everyone else. It was only after becoming a bit acquainted that she moved on to the business at hand.

Cassandra and Tomás know each other well, and respect each other greatly. Their differences and their respect for those differences have played a large part in the successes they have enjoyed. They have come to appreciate that their differences in opinion and approach can be as much a strength as a weakness. Cassandra and Tomás learned that a critical part of their legislative conferences in Washington, D.C. was the effort they made to help those who participated to build honest relationships both prior to and during their trips.[31] During the legislative conferences, they gained practical experience in effectively engaging citizens from across the country in the governing process. Because they themselves come from opposite sides of the political aisle, they were able to relate to a wide range of participants and help them discover common ground with one another.

Both also have had mediation training, which they jokingly relate has been useful in their own working relationship. Their partnership and the Institute's continued growth and success offer living proof of the wisdom and practical application of the Rules for Civility they present in this book. Each of the rules shared earlier in this book arose out of their experiences and work with the Church in Washington and the Institute. The rules also evince their deep and abiding Christian faith, and the knowledge they have gained from their seminary studies as well as from their experience as pastors.

One proof of the effectiveness of the rules developed by the Institute is evident in the close working relationship Cassandra and Tomás enjoy as the Institute's co-founders. As their story demonstrates, Cassandra and Tomás have overcome real differences on important issues in the interest of civility. Their story illustrates in concrete form the value of knowing yourself and listening to others with very different beliefs with respect while trusting their commitment to the relationship you are building as you dialogue about tough issues. The results of struggling with their differences with respect have enriched both their lives. Working beside those with whom we have an established relationship gives us critical knowledge about what makes them "tick." Such knowledge helps as we tackle tough issues, whether we reach consensus or simply respectfully agree to disagree.

Quart Graves

(as told by Quart Graves, retired former Vice-President of a large oil company)

My participation in the Church in Washington conferences in Washington, D.C. led by Cassandra and Tomás definitely changed my perception. I found the trips extremely interesting, perhaps because I had had some experience working with federal agencies. However, my previous experiences had been very narrow and focused. The church groups did a lot of work before the trips to identify national issues on which they wanted to advocate a position. The trips were a great exercise in consensus building. The groups included individuals from different backgrounds. Although we shared a common faith and all came from Southeast Texas, that was about as far the commonalities went. There were Republicans and Democrats. There were people who had never voted and people who had extensive involvement in civic participation. The effort required to reach consensus was a real exercise in constructive dealings among people who have disagreements and different understandings.

The goal was to reach consensus positions without those participating compromising their own beliefs until the final result became meaningless. With authentic, agreed-upon positions, the participants could go to their Congressional Representatives and say this is a consensus opinion from a group of individuals from many churches. The Congressional Representatives listened, especially when participants visited their own representatives individually. The trips were also a useful experience in constructive lobbying, and even with my background of working with federal agencies, they improved my knowledge of how government works.

An example of how those experiences have continued to help and influence me specifically occurred when my wife and I took our 14 year-old granddaughter to Washington, D.C. This young woman is bright and precocious. Both of her parents are teachers. We decided as long as we were going to Washington, D.C., we would make the trip a learning exercise for her. We decided to focus on the No Child Left Behind Act. We spent time searching for information on the Internet. The No Child Left Behind Act was 700 pages long, so we obtained a 10 page summary. We also went to the National Education Association and obtained their position papers, and our granddaughter talked to her teachers at school.

When we arrived in Washington, D.C., my wife and I and our granddaughter talked with a young aide to Senator Kay Bailey Hutchison. The aide had worked with the Senator on the No Child Left Behind Act. The meeting turned into a give and take situation. Our granddaughter had prepared ten questions, but when the aide realized that this young woman had done some homework before the meeting she began pumping *her* for information. The meeting was a wonderful experience. After the meeting ended, my wife and I told our granddaughter, "Now you know how a lobbyist works because you just were one."

When you know yourself and have done your homework, you may find as Quart Graves' young granddaughter did, that others are more likely to listen to you with respect regardless of differences in age, experience or beliefs. Though he had experience working with federal agencies, it was through his participation in the Church in Washington program that Quart gained additional first-hand experience about how our government works for ordinary individuals. Transformation occurs when we venture out of our comfort zones and open ourselves to new experiences and perspectives.

Chuck Seidel

(as told by Chuck Seidel, a former research scientist and educator at a medical school in Texas, a Presbyterian elder, and a member of the Planning Committee for the Church in Washington trips)

Regarding civility, I learned that we have to learn where the other person is coming from. We need to know this and be willing to learn and read in areas we don't want to learn about in order to be able to have a discussion. If I just have my position and you have yours, we can't have a discussion. I need to learn more about how you got to your position. I learned that all Presbyterians don't think alike--even those from the same part of Texas. I would find myself thinking that some people have ideas so very different from mine, and I couldn't understand how they could think such things. In other words I wondered how someone I respected for other reasons could have such a different view from mine. This effort takes time, and the process has to be one of conversation. We can't shout and learn this. A lot of the Sunday morning news shows are about how fast and loudly people can talk. I find them useless in promoting either conversation or understanding in the way that civility makes possible.

As Chuck Seidel's story illustrates, learning to work with those of different opinions requires listening with your strength, mind and heart.

Mary Holcomb
(as told by Mary Holcomb, a receptionist for a small manufacturing company in East Texas.)

The trips I took to Washington, D.C. with the Church in Washington Program were a learning process. The experiences taught me to talk effectively about my political convictions. The program was terrific. We met with my representative, Sheila Jackson Lee, both times that I went to Washington. On one occasion, Representative Lee met with us during a House Judicial Committee meeting. She slipped out of the meeting and met with us in a room adjacent to the Justice Committee Chamber. She was very gracious. One of our group, Mike, had worked with the Housing and Urban Development Administration and was in charge of a housing unit for low income individuals. He was very knowledgeable about his issue. We were able to listen as he spoke directly with Representative Lee. I thought of this conversation when I learned recently that Representative Lee had helped establish a project for housing. She appeared on television speaking about a project for using federal funds to help with housing for the poor in Houston. I was sure Mike's conversation had had an effect.

The first time I went to Washington, I was scared to death. One man in our group on one of the trips was focused on world health. His whole purpose for joining us was to help people before they got sick. He went to Washington to advocate for his cause with government officials, but others on the trip learned as they went. I was one of those. I didn't have the knowledge or experience to advocate in the way some of the others did, but I learned. We had to choose topics in which we were interested. I picked the United Nations. Another member of the group worked with me to write up points for discussion. Suddenly I was involved in Advocacy 101.

My experiences on the trips have affected me in many ways. When I heard Senator Santorum, Republican U.S. Senator for Pennsylvania, share his views on abortion on one of the Sunday TV talk shows, I wrote a letter thanking this Senator for his viewpoints. I later learned that he was someone from a different political party than mine. Before the trips to Washington, I might have paid more attention to his party affiliation than what he had to say, but now I try to listen to what people are saying. I remember that Republican President Reagan and the Democratic Speaker of the House, Rep. Tip O'Neill, used to disagree about everything, but were still able to socialize with one another. It seems like in the past, representatives used to disagree with each other and then later they socialized together. What a shame that it seems like this does not happen any more.

At the same time, I'm much more in tune with who represents my viewpoints. And I contact them. I sign petitions online all the time, or send a letter. Cassandra has taught me that if I want to say something to President Bush the best way is by fax or e-mail. I write letters now too. I am still more comfortable with phone calls and letters than with speaking to my representatives directly, but I am becoming more active. Abortion is one issue on which I have strong beliefs. When we went to Washington, I took information to each Senator's aide. That was a big step for me. I received letters afterwards from Senators Gramm and Hutchison.

My experiences with the Church in Washington and the Institute have encouraged me to be more positive in tone and to speak about my beliefs rather than focusing on what I think my listener is doing wrong. This is what the Institute promotes. I now enjoy learning about others and speaking to them with respect. I think it is wonderful when I can talk to someone with different beliefs. At work now, I have regular conversations with CEOs, truck drivers, co-workers and others, and it's fun to hear their different opinions. I learn a lot.

Mary Holcomb's story demonstrates that learning to express your beliefs with civility can be empowering and enrich your knowledge as you listen to others with different positions. Mary's life has been enriched and transformed because she's learned to engage in dialogue with people who think differently than she does.

Kathy Nobles
(as told by Kathy Nobles, a member of the Planning Committee for the Church in Washington trips)

One of the things that stands out in my mind about the first trip I took to Washington, D.C. was the Sunday when I had the opportunity to go to the Holocaust Museum. Our group was spending several days learning about and promoting civility in government through our contacts with each other and our federal representatives. Visiting the Holocaust Museum with this particular trip as a background made a big impression. I saw in a new way that if we do not treat each other with respect, we begin to think "I'm better than you are," and are soon dehumanizing others. The horrors that can come from this are evidenced by the Holocaust Museum. I see the risks from lack of civility as a reason for all people to be involved and present in Washington-- reminding those who serve us to treat each other with respect.

Another example of the horrors of treating each other uncivilly occurred a couple of months after this first trip to Washington, D.C. A group in our town asked a city council member from Jasper, Texas to talk about the racially motivated murder there of an African-American man that had occurred in his city. This story received major national press coverage. The city council member said that had the churches and other concerned people not been able to meet and talk with each other civilly after the murder, the whole area might have exploded in violence. His town had walked the narrow line between civil behavior and violence and had come through by being in caring dialogue with one another.

Civility matters. Most of the time when you mention the government, people throw up their hands and claim we can do nothing about it. So can we do something?

Our trips were not always completely successful. One individual we met, who is no longer in office, was a Representative from East Texas. He had a high striped collar, his boots were resting on his desk, and he had a big cat in his lap. He was leaning back in his seat, and I felt like he was just waiting for us women to get through with him so he could go have some lunch. Every time he went off on what sounded to me like a platitude, I would try to bring him back to where he stood on the issues in which we were interested. I don't think he cared why our small group from East Texas was there, even though we were his constituents. I was reminded once again that we can control only our own actions, and not those of others, and yet I believe that civility breeds civility and is important to hold on to.

On the other hand, many of our Congressional officials really welcomed us. We were talking with Senator Kay Bailey Hutchison on the steps of the Capitol and one of her aides came up to remind her she had three minutes to make it to a meeting. She said, "If you have time, you might be interested in what I'm getting ready to participate in." We followed her for about ten minutes through the Capitol and ended up in Senator Strom Thurmond's palatial office at the top of the Capitol

Building. It was one of the finest rooms imaginable! Senator Hutchison was participating in a ceremony honoring the men who helped form the Tuskegee Airmen. During World War II, at the time this group was formed, African-Americans were not allowed to join the Air Force. They were finally allowed to form their own group. About 10 or 15 of the men who had been involved in that group were there along with some other dignitaries. Senator Hutchison participated in that ceremony, and we were allowed to watch. It was an honor to be there.

One of the things that impressed trip participants was how hard everyone involved with the government in Washington works. Some folks seem to think our representatives just go to Washington to party. We saw how busy and overloaded they and their staffs are. We received numbers of handouts and papers before and during the trips. We knew that people had to write them and read, understand and act upon the information. The experience has increased my respect for the individuals who are working in our government. Even when I didn't agree with them, I was impressed with their dedication. There was never the time to get all the information I wanted from the representatives I met.

The trips taught me that the average person can plug into the system and use it to affect an issue he or she cares about. Sometime after those conferences, a social worker in our area presented a program about problems feeding children during the summer because of the federal cutbacks to a program sponsored locally by the Episcopal Church. Folks on mission committees in the different area churches responded. We were going to start giving peanut butter sandwiches at the church to hungry kids. We were told we might be feeding maybe 400 kids a day, so we realized we needed help, and federal funding was a possibility.

We ended up doing a professional presentation to the school board, who at that time were under the gun and trying to pass a building bond. It was in their best interest to generate goodwill in the community. By voting for the summer food program they could improve their image and help the bond process along. They approved the program, and we ran it for five years. During that time we went from serving 8,000 children to serving 16,000 hungry kids at three feeding sites. Had I not had the experience from the trips to Washington, D.C. of knowing I could hang in there and explore the system and the guidelines and competently work with all that, I'm not sure I would have supported and promoted this program. We had to have some knowledge and experience. In Washington I had learned one person can make a difference by recruiting others to tackle a problem together.

It has been an easy and logical follow up for me to be a member of the Institute. I think the forums sponsored by the Institute with college and high school students are fantastic. I was at one at Sam Houston University where there was a really good response from the more than 400 students who participated. The students came to get the promised class credit, but they stayed to learn. The students had good questions, and they were getting straight answers from the U.S. Representatives who were there. Listening to them as they came out of the forum talking about what was going on and being interested was refreshing. One of my dreams would be to expand the forums and involve not only college and high school students, but others from the community so that people could listen and learn and get involved.

Kathy's story demonstrates that numbers count. Groups of individuals working together can make a difference. Her story also illustrates that being an advocate for one's community can make a remarkable difference in people's lives.

Esther Crosby
(as told by Esther Crosby, a member of the Planning Committee for the Church in Washington trips)

During the trips to Washington, D.C. as we visited with our Senators and Congressional Representatives, we experienced civility in some offices but not in others, though we always did our best to display it ourselves. The idea was always that conference participants should try to reach a consensus on what we felt were the important things to talk about with our elected officials. That gave us an opportunity to practice our civility and consensus building skills. Sometimes it was really hard. This work was our introduction to politics and an opportunity to see politics in action. The 90's were particularly contentious political times in Washington, D.C., so these trips that modeled civility were particularly attractive.

Since that time, I have been to three of the Congressional Student Forums sponsored by the Institute. It's an interesting process to watch. The young people don't know what is going to happen, but they become energized as they find out. In some situations the kids are given extra credit by their professors for showing up. One forum at North Harris Community College in the Houston area was held on a Saturday afternoon. There were over 200 young people there. The students asked questions, which the two Congressional

Representatives answered in the form of dialogue rather than debate. Jane Ely, an editorial writer for the <u>Houston Chronicle</u>, wrote a wonderful editorial about civility after attending that forum and commended the Institute for its work.

Since the trips to Washington, D.C., my perspective has changed. My awareness of government is much higher. I now look at the paper regularly to see how Congress votes. I am comfortable picking up the phone and calling about something I do or don't like or sending an e-mail to my elected representatives. I found in Washington that the Representatives were anxious to hear what we had to say. They are bombarded by groups with specific agendas, and it is important for them to hear from more main-stream people. I feel more comfortable expressing myself now that I know a little more about our government and the system. I realize now that no matter what their political thinking, our elected officials do not have an easy life. They perform difficult and demanding work.

The trips to Washington, D.C. opened a new world for me. Because of the trips, I am applying what I have learned about the rules for civility in my everyday life. I am serving on the governing board of my church for the second time. I'm an upfront kind of person, and my experiences with the Institute have strengthened that approach in my work with the governing board. I have also learned civility doesn't work on everyone. People have to be comfortable with themselves and have enough understanding of their own motives to be willing to negotiate with others who have a different philosophy and not take conflict personally. Today, too many of us take things too personally. Why can't we discuss issues any more without demonizing each other? It's a major problem. A general lack of civility throughout our culture supports such negative attitudes, and we have allowed that to happen. I believe we can return to civility, politeness and kindness, without weakness. By teaching an awareness of the current negative climate and the skills needed to overcome it, the Institute is helping to make that possible. The Institute is a small voice, but it's growing stronger, and it needs to be heard.

Esther's story illustrates that knowing oneself is important in developing an appreciation for others. Working issues through together, if possible, is a positive development in any conflict situation.

Rebecca Reyna
(as told by Rebecca Reyna, an employee of the City of Houston, Texas)

I made three trips to Washington, D.C. with Tomás and Cassandra. During the first trip, when one of our elected representatives refused to see us, I got on the phone and called and made appointments. I told the representative's office, "You have to see us. You're our only representative." And the meetings were scheduled. This was the birth of my political action approach. I had never been really verbal before, but Tomás and Cassandra nurtured my ability to speak out. The first trip to Washington was an opportunity for me. They held my hand and walked me through it. By the end of the trip, Tomás said he was ready to find me a job in Washington.

Tomás and Cassandra are good at building consensus and mediating. I was younger and had more liberal views than others on the trips on some issues, but more conservative views on others. I had no gray hair when I started. Working in the social work field gave me a different perspective than some others on the trips. On one trip an issue on which group members tried to reach a consensus was a proposed gas tax increase. Some of the wealthier members of the group supported this. I spoke up about my clients for whom that would be a real hardship. Others listened respectfully. That experience really empowered me. I learned I had a voice in a room with people who were older and more educated. I learned I had something to offer as well. I learned that people would listen. I had an opinion and could contribute to the discussion.

Now, I see the Congressional Student Forums sponsored by the Institute as a way to provide young people with the empowerment I've experienced through the Institute and the earlier trips I made to Washington, D.C. Their experiences at the forums allow them to see that politicians will listen, and they are able to experience politics in a new way.

My favorite memory of my first Washington trip is of an older, retired gentleman with whom I did not see eye-to-eye. "English Only" was one of the first topics on which we disagreed. My Spanish is not really good. My mom says I speak like a *gringa*. I heard it at home, but I did not grow up speaking Spanish. So I'm not fluent. This gentleman strongly believed that when people live in this country, they need to speak English. His idea seemed to be that if you don't speak English you are less American and somehow unpatriotic. I told him, "Wait a minute! My dad speaks Spanish, and he fought in WWII for this country." We butted heads, and Cassandra had to really work with me that evening. Cassandra's room was really the debriefing room. Cassandra and Tomás came up with ways that we could bridge the gap between us. By the end of the trip this gentleman was buying me a drink, and we were friends. What helped us make that change was talking and sharing experiences. I listened to him and came to understand where he was coming from. It was basically just good communication. Too often we get so caught up in, or invested in, our own opinions that we can't put them aside long enough to have a dialogue. I came to see it was okay that he had different opinions. He was exposed to a different viewpoint, and, while he probably still has the same beliefs, we talked with each other and learned to respect each other.

I remember a phone call from Tomás--not my first one from him of this sort. He told me, "God is calling, and you have to listen." Tomás and Cassandra shared their dream of setting up an organization that would bring more civility to all our lives. When I was asked if I would join them, I jumped on board. As the Institute has grown and gained members, it has been a joy to see the Congressional Student Forums take place. The idea is that behavior trickles down. If our leaders and our executives are not going to be civil and show good manners, how can we expect our youth to exhibit civility? Yet if you sit down and talk with our youth about some of the basic ideas that the Institute has and show them how to apply these ideas they become excited.

My experiences with the Institute have made me more aware of politics and of broader issues that I probably didn't pay attention to before. My involvement on the Congressional level, during the trips to Washington, D.C., and the idea that I can make a difference and have a voice, have led me into other activities such as my current job with the City of Houston.

Tomás and Cassandra still go to Washington, D.C. every year for the Institute. I went with them again about a year ago, and they wore me out. They had added a day to the schedule. It took all three of us to handle the appointments they had scheduled. I wore the hose off the bottoms of my feet! I told Tomás and Cassandra they were nuts with their schedules. I learned that no one on the Hill wears fancy shoes. After my experience during my last trip there I understand why.

I have gained confidence. Now when approaching a representative, I no longer think, "Why would this person listen to me? What would I have to offer that this person would listen to? How could I help matters?" For me that is the biggest change to come from my time with the Institute. I'll call people now and talk with them or go up to them and talk with them and not be intimidated because they are Congressional Representatives or Senators.

From the trips to Washington, D.C. and our efforts to reach consensus I have learned to take a deep breath and count and then try to look at things from another perspective. My experiences with the Institute remind me to be civil. I have learned it's okay if someone doesn't have the same opinions I do. I can still work with them.

Recently a City Council member visited my boss, and she was less than civil. But being involved in the Institute has taught me that I have to overlook such comments. I have learned that I still have to work with rude people, and I can still be civil. So instead of getting upset, I just laughed at what this Council Member had said, and then she turned around and smiled. My boss laughed too. The change in her attitude made us less defensive and helped me to understand why she was upset. Sometimes it is hard to be civil because people have very strong opinions, and they are very passionate about them. I'm glad that I had my involvement with the Institute before I began working in government. My involvement with Cassandra and Tomás has helped shape my ideas about politics, about whom I will respect and for whom I will work.

The Institute has humanized all politicians to me, and I now know that no elected official is more than human. They shouldn't be in a position where they think they don't need to listen. They need to remember they work for us. If we don't talk with them, they sometimes forget they are public servants. My boss is not that way.

The Institute sends out quotations about civility via e-mail to their members each month. I copied them off and sent them to my boss during the election campaign, and he put them up on his wall. Because of the Institute, I had come to realize the importance of the values of the people who represent us. I know if I'm going to be involved in politics, civility has to be part of my approach, just as it must be in any job.

The Institute has helped me realize that involvement matters. There are enough good people out there, but we really have to fight for those good voices to be heard, because there are also ugly voices out there. Politicians should not just be doing what is good for the groups that give them the most support. We should be able to come up with outcomes that are best for everyone, and in order to do that, everyone needs to participate. Knowing my ideas can be heard is important to me.

Through my experiences with the Institute, I have learned how to build consensus, but I still struggle every day to remind myself to work at doing so. I have also learned I have a voice, and how to use it responsibly. When I think about the current political climate, I sometimes want to run away and hide. Why would good people want to be involved and run for office? There are so many good people in public service, but they often become discouraged because of the climate that exists. We're losing a lot of people because of the hostile climate in which they must work. If civility weren't an issue, we would lose fewer good people.

Rebecca's story illustrates that one is powerful, and that listening is important, especially in discussions with those with whom we disagree.

CONCLUSION: HOPE FOR THE FUTURE. HOW DO YOU BECOME A PARTICIPANT RATHER THAN A BYSTANDER?

"Silence is not inaction. It is doing something; silence is acquiescence."
Rabbi Robert Marx

"Do what you can where you are with what you have."
Theodore Roosevelt

One of the things Cassandra and Tomás tried to do when they took groups to Washington, D.C. was to impress upon the group that Washington, D.C. was their town. As American citizens we have ownership of our capital in a way that is unique, valuable, and rare in this world. Cassandra and Tomás would point out various features in the Capitol building and remind them that this beautiful staircase is yours. They knew from their own experiences in Washington, D.C. that nothing else can stir your heart with a sense of the grandeur of our experiment in democracy quite like the experience of walking down the marble halls of the Capitol where our elected representatives meet. President Andrew Jackson reminded the country of this in a very concrete way when he opened the doors of the White House and invited the public in. Walking the halls of Congress is a visible reminder that we the people *are* the government in this country. If we want the process to be more civil, we can accomplish that. But we have to do that for ourselves, because we are the only ones who can change this process, which belongs to us and includes each of us.

What difference does all of this make in our everyday lives? Where do we go from here? Applying the ten rules offered by the Institute to our governing process can transform the American way of governing, as well as our experiences in our local neighborhood civic organizations, places of business and religious groups. While this book has approached this topic from the perspective of our interactions in the public square, these rules also work well in other settings. It is important to keep in mind that whatever we try to negotiate is dynamic and is affected by the expectations of those involved in the dialogue. Negotiation, like life itself, is a process. Our need to negotiate with others with whom we differ is an ongoing task. Parents understand this concept in their gut.

Tomás and Cassandra were able to work with the groups they took to Washington, D.C. in their early days as advocates on social justice issues because they had to work through the tough issues between themselves. That made it easier for them to work with others who also disagreed. They were able to help others learn the skills exemplified by the rules they offer in this book because they had to learn these rules themselves in order to work together. Differences are enriching, but they had to work hard to learn to appreciate that reality. Their hard work in understanding their differences made demonizing each other no longer an option because they found some of what the other had to say on specific issues made sense. Because Tomás and Cassandra had learned how to dialogue effectively themselves in their working relationship, it has made it easier for them to teach others.

As we begin to put the rules offered in this book into practice in our communities and daily lives, it helps to remember when contacting elected officials with a request, not to assume anything. That means do not assume that people in the same office talk with each other, that they received the information, or even that they are having a good or a bad day. We must individually be willing to carry the process along on issues that are of importance to us. If we do not pursue our issue, it will fall through the cracks. We have to help people do their jobs by being a resource for them. Our request is our responsibility, not theirs. Democracy only works when people get involved and stay involved. Too many people become offended by the process, or lack of one, and assume their request has been moved along by others. Then they become angry when they discover this has not happened, and that gets the process further off track. Elected officials and their staff work more effectively with nice people as is true of all of us. Most of them try very hard to listen and do a good job. They can do a better job with our help.

In talking with others we have learned that many today seem to feel under attack, whether liberal or conservative, and their reaction is to hunker down and say nothing. Even people who believe their opinions are middle-of-the-road are having this reaction. Not all are interested in enhancing civility in our society. Some elected officials seem to thrive on negative interactions and view civility as a weakness. They are concerned that civility blurs the differences between the political parties and is thus inappropriate. They seem willing to work with and be civil only to members of their own party. Other citizens seem to have trouble with the concept of civility as well.

We deserve better than the current state of the public square, but we are also complicit in the current situation. Each individual citizen deserves part of the blame for the sorry state of dialogue in our civic life. We have the power to change what we do not like. Alone we can make an impact. Joined together with other citizens who are also interested in civility, regardless of their political views, we can have an even greater impact and foster change for the better. That is why joining an organization such as the Institute is so very important. Every member counts.

We need to recall and reclaim the best of those original ideals on which this country was founded. We need to remember who we are as a people. We need to rekindle our belief in and understanding of representative government. Richard J. Mouw argues that the divisive problems we face in our public square are a direct result of our amnesia. We have forgotten the importance of community and what that means, and we have also forgotten the importance of citizenship and the value of each individual in this national community in which we live.[32] Mouw contends that we have lost sight of the benefits of civility in the public square. In our desire to become closer to one another we have made the mistake of confusing political relationships with personal ones and as a result insist on working out public matters based entirely on personal feelings.[33] Mouw insists that this failure to differentiate our personal from our public selves is eerily similar to the problems faced by mental patients in their encounters with society, an unnerving, but thought provoking way of looking at our current interactions in the public square.[34]

The current focus on the lack of civility in our interactions in the public square can also be seen as evidence of the importance of community to humans. We are social beings in need of interaction with each other for sustenance. We seek a sense of true community, not one where our differences are stamped out, but one where those differences enrich the whole, as a variety of flowers adds beauty of color and scent to a bouquet. This type of community can be experienced in the public space when we are able to engage in effective dialogue about issues on which we differ.[35] In order to attain this type of community, the type which this book is designed to foster, we must learn to approach dialogue with a deep appreciation for the sanctity of our fellow citizens and a clear-eyed and humble assessment of our own limitations.[36]

We know change comes slowly, but the fact that we have yet to create a perfect version of such a community here and now does not make that ideal any less worthy of earnest attempts to achieve that goal. And there are dangers in not trying. If we seek that goal and watch for and celebrate signs of this community formed by civility in the public square, we will glimpse perfection, perhaps when we least expect it. One has only to read the stories included in this book to begin to understand that promise. May we go forward with dedication to creating and fostering true civility in our homes, communities, and nations. The rewards will be immediate and tangible. Our future will be richer as a result of our combined efforts.

APPENDIX 1: ABOUT THE INSTITUTE

THE INSTITUTE FOR CIVILITY IN GOVERNMENT

The Challenge
It would appear that being disengaged from the system is the norm, and that harshly criticizing one another without engaging in civil dialogue is perfectly acceptable. We wonder what has happened to the art of creative problem solving and compromise, not only among elected officials, but within our communities as well. What are the standards we are setting for future generations? Why can't we treat one another with civility any more?

The Organization....
Incorporated Sept. 1997, the Institute for Civility in Government began functioning as an organization in April 1998. Membership is available for an annual fee of $25 for adults/$10 for students. Members receive quarterly newsletters and invitations to Institute events. Those who are on-line also receive monthly e-mail quotes.

Not a think-tank, and not a watchdog organization, we are an absolutely unique citizens' movement for civility, serving as a catalyst for change.
While many organizations promote civic participation, and some groups work to build community, the Institute for Civility in Government is unique in the way that we bring these concerns together. The Institute fosters civil governance by facilitating dialogue, teaching respect, and building civility.

The Co-Founders
Cassandra Dahnke and Tomás Spath organized and led legislative conferences in Washington, DC for seven years. With good working relationships with members of Congress on both sides of the political aisle, Cassandra and Tomás have experience in engaging local citizens in the governing process effectively. They have spoken before faith communities, civic organizations, schools, conferences, and Members

of Congress. Both have mediation training, along with significant experience working with community organizations.

Cassandra was raised in Corpus Christi, Texas and is a graduate of Texas Tech University and Austin Presbyterian Theological Seminary. She is a Presbyterian pastor.

Tomás was born to missionary parents and raised in Argentina, bringing a cross-cultural perspective to his work. He is a graduate of McCormick Theological Seminary and Gettysburg College. He is also a Presbyterian pastor.

Members

We all need the Institue to be out there facilitating dialogue, teaching respect, and building civility. In order to do that, the Institute needs you! Members of the Institute are people committed to working for greater civility within the governing process and society at large. They are students, clergy, homemakers, retired folk and business leaders. Their careers are as diverse as real estate, computer programming, accounting, teaching, engineering, insurance, retail, social work, and air traffic control. Many of our members volunteer their help at our Congressional Student Forums and other events.

As of the writing of this book, our membership draws from twenty-one states and the District of Columbia.

To learn how you can become a part of this movement contact the Institute and check out our website:

The Institute for Civility in Government
P.O. Box 41804
Houston, Texas, 77241-1804
713-444-1254 OR 281-782-4454
www.instituteforcivility.org
e-mail: info@instituteforcivility.org

Appendix 2: Books on Civility and Politics Reviewed by the Institute

1998
Politics for People by David Matthews
published by The University of Illinois Press, 1994
Politics for Dummies by Ann DeLaney
published by IDG Books Worldwide, Inc. 1995
Inside Congress by Ronald Kessler
published by Pocket Books, 1997

1999
The Politics of Meaning – Restoring Hope and Possibility in an Age of Cynicism
by Michael Lerner, published by Addison-Wesley Publishing Company, 1997.
The Power of Public Ideas, edited by Robert Reich
published by Harvard University Press, 1988
Civility – Manners, Morals, and the Etiquette of Democracy by Stephen Carter
published by Basic Books, 1998
Courage is Contagious by John Kasich
published by Doubleday, 1998

2000
A House Divided by Mark Gerzon
published by G.P. Putnam's Sons, 1996
If the Gods had meant us to Vote, They would have given us Candidates
by Jim Hightower, published by HarperCollins Publishers, 2000
The Argument Culture – Stopping America's War of Words by Deborah Tannen
published by The Balentine Publishing Group, 1998
Dialogic Civility in a Cynical Age by Ronald C. Arnett
published by State University of New York Press, 1999

2001
On Toleration by Michael Walzer
published by Yale University Press, 1997
God Views by Jack Haberer
published by Geneva Press, 2001
The Magic of Dialogue – Transforming Conflict into Cooperation
by Daniel Yankelovich
published by Simon & Schuster, 1999
Next – the Road to the good society by Amitai Etzioni
published by Basic Books, 2001

2002
The Uncivil War – The Rise of Hate, Violence, and Terrorism in America
by Stephen Singular, published by New Millennium Press, 2001
Chasing the Red, White and Blue – A Journey in Tocqueville's
Footsteps Through Contemporary America by David Cohen
published by Picador USA, 2001
The Passion of the Western Mind – Understanding the Ideas That
Have Shaped Our World View
by Richard Tarnas
published by Ballantine Books, 1991
The Art of Political Warfare by John J. Pitney, Jr.
published by University of Oklahoma Press, 2000

2003
The Spirit of Community – The Reinvention of American Society
by Amitai Etzioni
published by Simon & Schuster, 1993
The Tipping Point – How Little Things Can Make a Big Difference
by Malcolm Gladwell
published by Little, Brown, and Company, 2000, 2002
Nonviolent Communication – A Language of Compassion by
Marshall B. Rosenberg
published by Puddle Dancer Press, 1999
Jihad vs. McWorld – Terrorism's Challenge to Democracy by
Benjamin R. Barber
The Ballantine Publishing Group, 1995

2004
How to Speak, How to Listen by Mortimer Adler

Published by Touchstone of Simon & Schuster, 1983
The Character of Leadership: Political Realism and Public Virtue in Nonprofit Organizations
by Michael Jinkins, Published by Jossey-Bass Publisher, 1998.
Bowling Alone – The Collapse and Revival of American Community
by Robert D. Putnam, Published by Simon & Schuster, New York, 2000.

2005
Choosing Civility: The Twenty-five Rules of Considerate Conduct
by Dr. P.M. Forni, Published by St. Martin's Press, New York, New York, 2002.
Doing Democracy: The MAP Model for Organizing Social Movements
by Bill Moyer, JoAnn McAllister, Mary Lou Finley, and Steven Soifer, Published by New Society Publishers, British Columbia, Canada, 2001.
An Ethics for Enemies – Forgiveness in Politics
by Donald W. Shriver, Jr., Published by Oxford University Press, New York, 1995.
Leadership and Self-Deception – Getting out of the Box
by The Arbinger Institute, Published by Berrett-Koehler Publishers, Inc. San Francisco, 2000.

2006
turning to one another – simple conversations to restore hope to the future
by Margaret Wheatley, Published by Berrett-Koehler Publishers, Inc. San Francisco, 2002.
Hope Unraveled: The People's Retreat and Our Way Back
by Richard C. Harwood, Published by the Charles F. Kettering Foundation, Dayton,
Ohio, 2005.
The Values Divide by John Kenneth White, published by Chatham House Publishers of Seven Bridges Press, 2003.
Simple Truths on Values, Civility, and Our Common Good by Stephen Bauman, published by Abingdon Press, 2006.

APPENDIX 3: HOW TO CONTACT YOUR ELECTED REPRESENTATIVES AND GOVERNMENT AGENCIES

Though the speed of postal deliveries to Capitol Hill has slowed down considerably in the wake of terrorist attacks, being in contact with government officials is not difficult. Many phone books have a government section at the front called the "Blue Pages" that list local, state, and national government offices and phone numbers for that area.

The Internet provides not only a wealth of information, but the ability to be in touch via email. Virtually every department of the U.S. government has a website. In the case of Congress, you can find the websites for your Senators or Representatives by going to www.senate.gov or www.house.gov respectively.

Every member of Congress has a website that provides all the information you need about physical addresses of offices both in Washington, D.C. and back home in the district, as well as phone and fax numbers. Frequently staff information and office hours are posted as well. Every member of Congress has offices not only in Washington, but also back home in their districts. Often it is much easier to get an appointment close to home rather than traveling across the country. Additionally, many members of Congress host town hall meetings that are open to the public. This is quite possibly the easiest way for constituents to meet their elected officials.

To reach the President, go to www.whitehouse.gov, which gives guidelines for all communication with that office. If using the postal service, you can send your letters to:

The White House
1600 Pennsylvania Avenue NW
Washington, DC 20500

Additionally, you can be in touch with the White House via phone or fax through these numbers:

Comments: 202-456-1111
Switchboard: 202-456-1414
FAX: 202-456-2461

Be aware that due to the very high volume of communications, a response to your concerns may take time, but you will almost always get a response. Be patient, and consider the most effective way to be in touch. Knowing who has the authority and responsibility to deal with your issue or problem is extremely helpful. If you don't know, call an office and ask. Most Congressional offices have local or toll-free numbers for their constituents.

Be sure to follow through not only with your request, but with a response. Remember to say thank you to those who help and serve. It may be their job, but we should appreciate it nonetheless.

APPENDIX 4: CIVILITY: PAST AND PRESENT

*"We may please ourselves with the prospect of free and
popular governments. God grant us the way. But I fear that in
every assembly, members will obtain an influence by noise not
sense, by meanness not greatness, by ignorance not learning,
by contracted hearts not large souls. There is one thing, my
dear sir, that must be attempted and most sacredly observed
or we are all undone. There must be decency and respect and
veneration introduced for persons of every rank or we are
undone. In a popular government this is our only way."*
- John Adams

*"Our government is the potent, the omnipresent teacher. For
good or for ill, it teaches the whole people by its example."*
- Justice Louis Brandeis

Raymond Smock, Historian of the U.S. House of Representatives,
in a conversation with Richard Baker, Historian of the U.S. Senate,
noted that heated debates occur daily in Congress, but they are
generally carried out with civility according to strict parliamentary
rules. Those rules are designed to prevent reasoned debate from
degenerating into something much less formal and decorous.[37]

Smock noted there are those who have argued that U.S.
Congresses, especially since the 1980s, have evidenced a clear decline
in harmonious relations.[38] Those making this argument specifically
relate the decline to a reduction in civility in our society in general.
While there are examples of recent uncivil behavior to support their
argument, Smock expressed his preference for the current situation.
He says the current situation is healthier than it was in the early 19th
century when members attended sessions armed and were more
frequently involved in fist fights or duels.[39] Smock suggested that
perhaps the First Congress, which met from 1789 to 1791, is the
closest we have ever come to a "Golden Age." However, the First
Congress also had its critics.

From the perspective of the House Historian, Congress has always been subject to complaints. Sometimes the public has been even more critical of Congress than usual, and we appear to be in such a period at the present time. Smock related regular criticism of Congress in part to the healthy skepticism of government characteristic of a representative democracy, where power is centered in the people. He expressed concern not with the skeptics, but with those who become so cynical that they neglect to participate and do their part to make our system function. When general participation declines, he said, we are at risk for an increase of those the country's founders called "pretended patriots"--individuals who fill the vacuum left by the non-participants by proposing simple solutions to complex problems at the same time that they exaggerate the dangers of the present.[40]

In the United States of America, it sometimes appears the only way we are "United" is in support of our increasingly vitriolic political interactions. Voices of civility and moderation are too often drowned out in the shouting and shoving. Observers of our current political scene express concern that relations in the public square seem to be worse than they have ever been. Many of us worry where our democratic society is headed if the situation continues to deteriorate. Others argue that our current situation is better than at other times in our history when political disputes often turned violent. A better understanding of where we came from perhaps can help us better evaluate where we are and whether change in our interactions in the public square is indeed needed. A review of the actions of our forebears offers a useful and more realistic perspective on our current situation. A look at our history demonstrates that our predecessors in the public square also wrestled with each other, both verbally and otherwise, as they confronted difficult problems from a variety of viewpoints. The failure of our elected representatives to model perfect civility in their interactions is thus not a new occurrence.

Mark Juergensmeyer has suggested that societies that slide into such simplistic approaches tend to create enemies, or use those who make themselves available, to characterize political relations as a battle between good and evil. He suggests that not infrequently such a simplistic approach imagines a world filled with primary and secondary enemies. For those who see issues in terms of black and white, secondary enemies are often government authorities or those who suggest civil discourse. Since those who suggest civil discourse treat disputes as if they were rational differences about which reasonable people can disagree, they become enemies as well. They are seen as defending the primary enemy and refusing to see their society as engaged in some sort of cosmic battle.[41] The mind set which creates or makes use of real enemies of the society can result in actions ranging from incivility through violence to terrorism, all given free reign because those with more nuanced understanding refused to contribute to the public discourse.

As the House Historian has noted, the democratic process in this country has never been a perfect model of civilized discourse and courteous behavior, our rosy-hued view of our past history notwithstanding. Our government from the beginning has been composed of fallible human beings who are elected by others of the same species. Not only incivility, but also acts of violence have been a regular part of our history in the public square. Violent incidents in the U.S. Congress, and among members outside the confines of the House and Senate, have actually declined in the 20th century as compared to the 19th century. There have been many instances of such behavior in our history.[42] Vice President Aaron Burr's fatal wounding of Alexander Hamilton in a duel in 1804 is probably the most famous incident of political violence in our history. Following his retirement as Secretary of the Treasury in 1795, Hamilton led a faction of the Federalist Party in its opposition to President John Adams and his policies. Burr and Hamilton were rival politicians, and their duel grew out of their political disputes.[43] The incident, though notorious, was by no means unique.

Senator John Randolph of Virginia was elected to the U.S. Senate in 1825. There his intemperate language regarding the appointment of Secretary of State Henry Clay goaded Clay into challenging Randolph to a duel.[44] Dueling between members of Congress officially ended only after Rep. William Graves of Kentucky killed popular Representative Jonathan Cilley of Maine in a duel in 1838.[45] Mr. Smock pointed out that one particularly heated debate occurred in 1858, not long before the beginning of the Civil War. During the debate over the admission of Kansas to the Union, specifically over whether Kansas would be admitted as a free or slave state, two members of the House escalated their debate from insults to physical altercation. Suddenly, like the bench-clearing brawls all too common in today's sporting events, some fifty members of the House of Representatives erupted into fighting throughout the chamber. The Sergeant at Arms and the Speaker of the House were unsuccessful in their attempts to halt the violence on the floor. The melee ended when one member attempted to grab the hair of William Barksdale of Mississippi, but succeeded only in removing his wig. The mood changed abruptly from violence to hilarity as the members broke into laughter over the "scalping" of Representative Barksdale and ceased their brawl.[46]

Eugene L. Wolf, who has studied instances of legislative violence, has counted 31 hostile confrontations, primarily on the floor in Congress, and 34 duels or challenges.[47] Wolf noted that similar incidents have occurred at other levels of our government.[48] He has suggested that our early history was a setting in which political parties were embryonic. Party differences thus provided fewer possibilities for disagreement so, in an attempt to distinguish one party from another, political disputes often became personal in nature. Confrontations and duels arose out of real or perceived attacks on an opponent's character. Our current situation differs to some extent.[49] However, if we are indeed seeing an increase of incivility and personal attacks on political opponents in our own time, encouraging more civil interactions is a prudent way to avoid a possible return to the more violent confrontations of our past.

The House Historian also addressed concerns about gridlock in Congress. He noted that gridlock is a reality, but believes its deleterious effects have been exaggerated. Conflicts were deliberately built into our system of government through the checks and balances incorporated into the Constitution. As a result, discourse, especially in our current two-party system, may be especially polarized.[50] A dictatorship might streamline debate, but that is what the drafters of the Constitution sought to avoid. Mr. Smock observed that critics have tended, from the beginning, to judge Congress by the messiness of its process rather than by the results of that process.[51] He also suggested that our perceptions of the messiness of the Congressional process have not been helped by the availability of instant, live access to that process. Now rather than the weeks or months it sometimes took news to travel earlier in our history, we can experience the actions in Congress immediately. When, as now, the people whom Congress represents are evenly divided on how to proceed on many issues, it should be no surprise to find their representatives divided along the same lines. According to Mr. Smock, gridlock is a term generally used by those who are unhappy about specific legislation to imply that the process itself has ceased to function. The reality is that even though Congress may be at a standstill regarding specific issues, action is nonetheless generally ongoing on other important matters.[52]

The fact that our present situation is similar to other periods in our history should provide some comfort to observers of political interactions. In fact, given our history, it is reassuring to note that hostile confrontations in Congress today are notably less violent than such encounters in the past. However, though our current governmental representatives are not regularly engaged in duels or fist-fights on the floor of Congress, observers of our civic interactions are right to note that civility is in short supply and constructive dialogue is all too rare. The speed with which our technology presents us with incidents perhaps gives us a greater sense of urgency in the current situation. If the original members of Congress had a heated argument, it was not shown on television or instantly communicated online or publicly debated ad infinitum on radio and television talk shows. The argument was confined to the room in which members of Congress were meeting, and quite possibly not even reported in the papers. The immediacy and pervasiveness of media reporting in our time has shifted the landscape and expanded both the scope and the depth of influence of the actions of our elected representatives, both for good and for ill. Fair or not, the tone set by the behavior of our elected officials does grant a kind of permission to the rest of us to do the same.

Neither of our major political parties has been immune from outbreaks of juvenile behavior in our time. Tomás Spath remembers that shortly after the Republicans won the majority of the seats in the House of Representatives for the first time in many years, three evening newscasts began their broadcast with images of a Democratic Representative from Florida spitting on the Republican Representative who was the new Chair of the House Ways and Means Committee. Tomás recalls that the Florida Representative was angry because the Chair would not allow him to add an amendment to a bill that was going to the floor of the House for a vote. He further recalls that the Chair of the Committee commented that he had been watching the Democrats do things their way for many years and now it was the Republicans' turn. This incident was also instrumental in the creation of the Institute for Civility in Government as Tomás was so incensed by the spitting, replayed over and over on TV, that he called Cassandra and said "We have to do something". The Institute was born soon after. Other incidents of incivility in recent years have included physical altercations between various members of the House of Representatives in the Capitol Building. [53] More recently, a high ranking government official used an expression not generally heard in polite society, let alone on the floor of the U.S. Senate, as he addressed a Senator of the opposition. A former member of Congress who retired after 30 years of service told Cassandra and Tomás that when he began his time in Congress the 1-minute speeches allowed members at the beginning of each day were used to offer positive contributions and build up the membership and nation. Now those speeches have become a time to blast the opposing party and speak in divisive sound bites. This member co-sponsored a bi-partisan resolution, signed by 59 colleagues, to move the 1-minutes to the end of the day so that at least the House would not begin each day on a negative note. Though reviewed by the House Rules Committee, no action has been taken to move the 1-minutes, and many members still use them in less than civil ways.

APPENDIX 5: PARTICIPATION IN COMMON CIVIC LIFE

"I know of no safe depository of the ultimate power of the society but the people themselves, and if we think them not enlightened enough to exercise their control with a wholesome discretion, the remedy is not to take it away from them but to inform their discretion by education."
- Thomas Jefferson

"If adult Americans will not model civic responsibility, how can we expect our young people to be any different?"
- Richard Riley, Education Secretary, Clinton Administration

Some argue that incivility is driving people from the public square. In a report in advance of the 2004 general election, Bill Moyers reported that voter registration in the U.S. was up, but participation was down. He noted 60.3% of those old enough to vote did so in the 1964 election. By 2002 that percentage had declined to 54.7%.[54] Moyers also reported that a low percentage of voter participation is nothing new in the U.S. The percentage of eligible voters who actually voted in 2002 was similar to the percentage of participation when only white, land-owning males were eligible to vote. According to the Moyers report, the U.S. ranked 139th of 172 countries in voter participation based on statistics of elections from 1945 to 1998. These figures were based on the percentage of the voting-age population, not registered voters, who voted. According to the Moyers report, Italy ranked 1st in voter turnout with 92.5% of the voting age population voting, while 48.3% in the U.S. voted, just below Russia with 55% voting.[55] Some countries have approached the issue of voter non-participation by requiring their citizens to vote, though this has never been the rule in the United States. Belgium began this practice in 1892. Australia has had this requirement since 1924. Countries as diverse as Argentina and Switzerland also require voting. Penalties for noncompliance include fines and disenfranchisement.[56] Various countries have also experimented with other methods of simplifying voting, including voting by mail and allowing early voting, an option that has become more common in this country, and holds out the prospect for changing our election dynamics in some interesting ways.[57] Some observers suggest Internet voting as a possibility in the future.[58]

The U.S. Census Bureau, in a report looking towards the 2004 Presidential Election, provided statistics from prior elections. Voting trends by state show that the highest voting rates--approximately 70% in 2000--were in the District of Columbia, North Dakota, Wisconsin, Maine and Minnesota. Eighty-six percent of those registered to vote in 2000 actually voted in the presidential election that year. Of those who said they were registered, but did not vote, 21 percent said they were too busy or had schedule conflicts because of work or school.[59] Some experts express concern regarding the low participation rate, especially for young voters, who tend to vote in lower percentages than those who are older.[60] Others note that younger people may not be voting, but they are involved in activities to improve their communities.[61] Older voters, however, express fears that the failure of younger Americans to participate in political as opposed to community activities may effectively leave the running of the government to those with more extreme views who are more likely to be politically active.[62] The approach of today's younger voters is a change from the traditional approach of combining community activism with political activity. Some who are familiar with the downward trend in youthful voting patterns are concerned that younger voters fail to understand that political action can help to solve the community problems with which they are involved.[63] Not surprisingly, some of the young people disagree and believe their cynicism about the value of political involvement is well founded. They argue they are no different than older voters in their disenchantment with the current political situation in this country. They claim politics as currently practiced is at fault, not the younger generation[64].

Observers of the political scene differ regarding whether lack of voter participation is a problem. Andrew J. Glass decried the fact that citizens are not carrying out their civic duty at the ballot box, and they compare U.S. voter turn out unfavorably to that in Russia.[65] Some worry that the decline in participation in our representative form of government is an ominous trend that is related to a generally jaundiced view of our elected officials, whose reputations are dismal. Our limited contact with our representatives is cited as a reason for this lack of trust in our elected officials. We also suffer from the perception that only those who contribute money can obtain access to those who govern.[66] Lee Mortimer argues that more fundamental and systemic reasons are responsible for voter apathy and non-participation. He contends that people do not believe their votes count. According to this argument, most elections are not really contests. Incumbents have a tremendous edge. In presidential elections many states operate under winner-take-all rules for determining votes in the Electoral College. As a result the only real suspense regarding the outcome occurs in a few battleground states. Those, like Mortimer, who argue there is good reason for voter apathy insist that only when voters demand changes in the system from their elected officials will the political situation improve. [67] Matthew A. Crenson and Benjamin Ginsberg contend that lack of voter participation can be traced to the decline in the government's demand and need for citizen participation. They argue we have become consumers rather than citizens. We demand rights and benefits, but we fail to ask tough questions about government actions and to insist on the right to participate in our own government.[68] Robert D. Putnam, in his book *Bowling Alone,* has related a decline in political participation to a decline in overall civic and community involvement.[69]

The good news may be that, like worries that our political situation has never been so uncivil, worry about current voter non-participation is based on an overly optimistic view of a perfect past that never existed. In fact, in some ways, our voting situation is much improved over that of past times. During the 19th century, voting was not secret. Votes were often solicited and sometimes paid for by party bosses. The secret ballot was instituted only toward the end of the 19th century. Around the same time voters began to seek to become self-informed rather than rely solely on party loyalty also came to be accepted wisdom. Perhaps as we move into the 21st century, younger voters, with their lack of confidence in government and other traditional institutions and their willingness to volunteer to improve their communities, will develop their own new form of citizen participation to accomplish the improvements they seek in their communities.[70] Voting participation has tended historically to increase with age. That fact coupled with the intangible rewards experienced by those who do actively participate, such as a sense of contributing to their national and local communities, may be reason for optimism that even our disenchanted younger voters will eventually participate more actively in the political process.[71]

In order to persuade people to remain committed and to participate in our democratic system, however, we need to convince them that civility is possible. In our current political climate, people appear most interested in keeping a lower profile.[72] They worry about what active participation will cost them and their families, most especially those who consider public service as a vocation. Perhaps even more importantly, they think they will not be heard and cannot make a difference. The experiences of those involved with the Institute demonstrate that while this is an understandable fear, it is not grounded in reality. Those who approach their elected representatives using the rules offered by the Institute can be heard and do make an impression.

Even Machiavelli was convinced that a whole society can evidence virtue in its culture and was further convinced that type of culture results in more civil interactions in the public square. In order for civic virtue to prevail, however, Machiavelli also believed that people needed to be actively involved rather than passive non-participants.[73] We have become so sanguine about our liberties and our democracy that we forget our nation is a new experiment in human history, one that has existed for less than 300 years, not long at all in the history of nations. We also take too little into account the fact that people in other countries travel great distances and endure great personal risk in order to cast their votes, a privilege too many of us take for granted. In the span of history we are an aberration, a new and very fragile experiment. Without our participation, there is no government of the people, by the people and for the people. Without active participation our elections could be cancelled for lack of interest. It has happened in the recent past. In 1997, the City of Wickett, Texas cancelled elections after only one candidate filed for the three seats up for reelection.[74] The tough reality is that, for democracy to work, the people who are the government in this society must participate.[75]

Experience in the workings of our democratic system teaches that political education is a two-way street. Citizen participation is important for the education of our elected representatives, as is citizen education by our representatives.[76] Cassandra and Tomás learned this lesson in their work with their own Congressional Representative while they were advocating regarding social justice issues. Even though the three of them often disagreed on particular legislation, they all shared a common concern about the issues. Cassandra said their representative taught her to look carefully for unexpected impacts legislation might have. And she and Tomás would sometimes ask him questions that he could not answer, forcing him to re-examine and challenge his own positions. They worked well together because they shared a respect for each other as well. They were willing to listen and to learn from each other and to continue in dialogue while they worked through their differences.

Tools for effective dialogue are crucial. The reality is that even those who want to be civil and participate in the process often do not know how to do so in the context of conflict over important issues. And that includes many elected officials and those who work for them. We can all benefit from concrete suggestions for how to proceed, such as the rules offered by the Institute. These rules present practical approaches to dialogue between groups and individuals with differing views. Practicing these rules will allow us to experience the rewards of effective participation in our representative government as well as the blessing of increased civility.

APPENDIX 6: STUDY GUIDE WITH QUESTIONS FOR DISCUSSION USING SUCCESS STORIES FROM OTHERS OUTSIDE THE INSTITUTE WHO HAVE MODELED CIVILITY.

This Appendix includes additional pieces about civility and questions for discussion. Lest you conclude that the rules for civility may work for those individuals who have been involved with the Institute, but not under other circumstances, read on to learn about others who have modeled civility in their communities. Perhaps one reason our world appears to be dominated by those who regularly exhibit uncivil behavior is that stories such as those that follow are not the type we generally hear on the news or read about on the front page. One way we can increase civility in our local communities and the world is by discussing and encouraging the sharing of stories such as these. The hope and inspiration they provide can energize us to work more diligently to promote civility in all of our encounters with our fellow human beings.

THE MORNING AFTER, BY LYNDA RAE (USED WITH PERMISSION)

I am president of our Home Owners Association. There are 176 town homes built around three large parks, all enclosed by a wall that goes all around the complex. A block long drive featuring park-like grounds on both sides of the drive and in the middle island of the drive, greets you at the entrance. We have five large parks and a club house and pool which the Association must supervise. To add to the responsibility, the complex is now thirty years old. Irrigation systems, landscaping, walls, roads, lamp posts--all are at the point of needing to be replaced rather than repaired. Managing the complex is a huge responsibility, almost a full time job, between the landscaping, the repairs, and a large budget. In addition, the State of Nevada has very strict laws concerning homeowner associations. NSR 116, which governs Nevada Homeowner Associations is 59 pages of small print. I had to attend a class regarding the laws and then sign a legal document stating that I understood and would uphold them during my term as President.

When I was asked to run for the board, I had no idea what I was getting myself into. And then, I was voted in as President. So I now have the final vote, must sign every check, every legal document, conduct and answer at every board meeting for the actions of the board. I meet with lawyers on a regular basis. Any action comes by me first.

We have a rather diverse community. It is an older community in an older part of Las Vegas, which is growing rapidly. There are all levels of income in the community: lawyers, doctors, teachers, accountants, a large number of white collar workers and many blue collar workers. We also have very diverse ethnicity here: white, black, Hispanic, Asian and Eastern European. There are also a small number of retired persons who use their town homes as a second home, away from home. We have a small inner community of Hispanics who come here to work in the casinos and send money home to their families in Mexico. Most of these families do not speak English.

To add to the mix, the board is made up of five people, each of whom is voted in. In other words, I have to work with what the community gives me, and I have no say as to who is on my board. To say the least, it has been a very challenging and growing experience for me. The kicker is I don't receive one cent of pay. It is all volunteer work! Nevada will not allow any kind of compensation.

Board meetings are open to the public, and my first as President was a disaster: angry persons, yelling, cussing, and screaming. I was appalled. Everyone hated everyone. No one wanted to listen. "Get these damn people out of here," "The teenagers have taken over the pool, fill it up with rocks. Get rid of them," "I won't swim in a pool with a person of another race." "The houses on the east side get all the good stuff." "Back in the old days we did ....," "What does the board do with all that money?" It went on and on. Being a pacifier by nature, I tried to reason with people and extend a spirit of good will. I think the noise was so loud that they didn't even know I was saying anything. I finally called the meeting to an end.

Then I had to face my worst critics: the other four members of the board. They spent another hour of my time telling me what I should or should not have done. I felt like an actress, getting her reviews after her first performance. The reviews were bad!

The morning after that first meeting I awoke very depressed. I was going to resign. That was all there was to it. I was not cut out for this kind of stuff. I did not want to waste my time listening to this. "Let someone else do it," I said, "Just let's see what they can do." However, another side of me, a very stubborn side of me, started to whisper-- Don't let them beat you. You're not a quitter. You can do this. Show them all! Bad attitude, I know, but I gave into it. The thought of failure was very distasteful to me.

So, I sat down that morning, the morning after, and made a list of my observations.

1. Very angry people
2. Very diverse board members, all with an agenda of their own
3. Very well meaning--but totally lacking in knowledge of the situation--President

At first I laughed at my list. It didn't take much insight to record what I saw. But then I took a second look. Looking at the three observations, one thing jumped out at me. In one respect the three groups were the same. All had a need to express themselves. The problem was a board meeting was not the right forum. There was not enough time, and nothing could be addressed unless it was on the agenda. It would also help for the board to appear united, at least in public. Okay, in simple terms--I needed a forum for the homeowners to vent. I needed a forum for the board to express their individuality and solutions. I needed a forum in which I could interact with all of them and discern the problems. Wow, that's a lot of forums.

I realized that I would need to give up some of my precious time to do this. I decided to establish Monday as Open Door Night. From seven to nine p.m., every Monday I would be at the club house. The door would be open and any one could come in and talk about anything. It would be a one on one kind of situation. People would have a chance to vent on a personal level, tell me how they felt and why. I would have a chance to explain the laws and rules that govern the board, and we both would try to find a solution to the situation. I did not require the board members to attend. I didn't even ask the board about doing this. I just announced that I was going to do it, and they were certainly welcome to come at any time.

The first Monday Open Door Night, I arrived at the club house and found the whole board waiting for me. I wasn't surprised. I knew they were going to keep tabs on me. What did surprise me was the number of persons who showed up during the two hours, never in a large group, but one, two or three at a time. Most were just walking by. One young couple came and showed us their new little baby. And the board started talking: some business, but mostly idle chatter, little things that had happened to them, etc.

For the past year, I have been at the club house every Monday night from seven to nine. These Monday nights have turned into something very enjoyable for me. I have a wealth of new friends because of them. First, every member of the board has become a good friend. We have all come to understand our differences, to be more tolerant of them, and more importantly to find our common ground. A year ago I would never have thought this possible, since we are all very different from one another.

I have also discovered the trouble makers. We have about 15 of them in our community. For them, nothing is right. They are always going to sue over something, and on and on. I just listen to them. I tell them I appreciate their concerns, but I have a job to do that is dictated by Nevada State Law. Some of them didn't believe me at first, so I decided to purchase a number of the NSR 116 books and have them available at the Monday night meetings. When one of these characters gets going, I dig out a book, find the paragraph that relates to the issues at hand, highlight it and hand it to them. I tell them they are welcome to have the book if they promise they will read it. Most of them read the paragraph and return the book. Then I ask them what they think I should do. This usually calms them down and starts a dialogue with them.

At least four of these people have become my good friends. One feisty old Italian woman in her 80's, who is very spry and has a sharp tongue, fixes my husband Joe and me a meal every week or so. She calls him and tells him "Linda needs to rest, she always looks so tired."

A young couple with heavy accents who can barely speak English came to the Open Door Night with a letter saying we were going to put a lien on the house because they were delinquent in payments. The man told me in his broken English he did not know what to do. This was a mistake. I really did not believe it was an error, since we keep excellent books, but I told him I would look into it and get back to him. I gave him my home phone number and told him to call my husband, who speaks fluent Spanish. I told him he could tell my husband in Spanish why he thought it was a mistake. That way Joe could interpret for me. As it turned out, it was a huge mistake, not by the association, but by the realtors and brokers who sold the couple the townhouse. Everything had been complicated by the language differences. We were able to resolve the problem and also discovered the couple had money coming back to them. Well, I became a hero and the word went out to the Hispanic community that the board is really not the enemy.

I could go on and on with stories of different people and their problems, but I will not. Suffice it to say, I believe the Monday Open Door Night has been a big success, not only for me, but also for the whole community.

Another thing has become a routine with me. Once a month, the morning after the board meeting, I do an assessment of the meeting and of my feelings concerning the community and the association. I take stock of the situation. I make mental notes of where we are in the grand scheme of the association and how we, as a board, are relating to the community. How can we improve and encourage others to feel a part of the association? I give myself a grade. I'm always striving to improve on my grade. There are a few things that have really made an impression on me concerning dealing with people of different opinions and backgrounds, dreams and desires.

One: Everyone needs a place, a forum, to vent anger and frustration: a safe and appropriate place.

Two: A good dialogue can be had if one becomes a good and very patient listener. The more you listen, the more you learn.

Three: Most people really do not understand the whole story, see the whole picture. After you have listened to them, you need to explain the way things work and why.

Four: Most people come up with the solution to their problems on their own. After you have listened to them and explained how things work and why, you just need to ask them how they would resolve the problem. They usually tell you a good way to do so after they vent and let their frustration out.

Five: All people need your respect. After a while of dealing with them, you usually find out they *deserve* your respect.

Six: There are a few bad apples. These you must deal with swiftly and firmly. Do not allow yourself to come down to their level. You lose when that happens.

Seven: Always be kind, considerate and even loving. Most respond in kind, but it sure makes you feel better, even if some do not reciprocate.

I am nearly through my year as president of the Home Owners' Association, but I am sure I will carry the things I have learned this year into other parts of my life. I think we all should have a Morning After session occasionally to reflect and rejuvenate. It works.

QUESTIONS FOR DISCUSSION:

- "I had no idea what I was getting myself into." For most of us venturing into a new dimension of civic life, this statement certainly applies, yet Lynda Rae did not let this stop her. Discuss both the positives and negatives of this situation.

- Ms. Rae makes clear that her position as Board president carried with it tremendous responsibility, both legal and otherwise. Comment on those responsibilities. Do situations such as this encourage or discourage people from engaging in their communities? Why?

- "I have to work with what the community gives me." Is this a plus or minus? How did this affect the situation and Ms. Rae's approach to it.

- Ms. Rae indicates the community was quite diverse. Is this a positive or negative? How did this contribute to the community's difficulties? How did it contribute to solutions?

- Ms. Rae was a volunteer. What factors encourage people to get involved? What discourages people from volunteering?

- Was Ms. Rae successful from the beginning? Why or why not?

- "I realized that I would need to give up some of my precious time to do this." Comment on the benefits of investing oneself in others.

- What was the result of Open Door Night on Mondays?

- What are some of the strategies that have helped facilitate dialogue?

- What did Ms. Rae learn that can be applied to other situations?

Dahnke/Spath/Bowling

THE MAYOR OF BRAZORIA, TEXAS

Meet Ken Corley, Mayor of Brazoria, Texas. He has served as mayor the past five years. Before then, he was a city councilman for two years. All along, he's managed his used car lot in this small city of Southeast Texas. He built a very nice record in those seven years. Through the leadership that he brought to his position, he was able to:

1. Build two parks in the city fully supplied with new playground equipment for families to enjoy,
2. His city was the first one to pass a sexual offender ordinance that restricts sex offenders to 1000 feet from where children gather. This ordinance being used as a model by many other cities in the state.
3. Build a new Junior High School (17 million dollars) as well as a new Texas Dow Employee Credit Union (3 million dollars).
4. Alleviate the flooding situation in one of the city's subdivisions.
5. Annex parts of the city to the North and to the South, which was the first time any annexation had taken place in 35 years.
6. Work on city drainage problems with the county, which required $350,000 raised cooperatively.
7. In conjunction with the county commissioner and county judge, replaced street signs, repaired drainage ditches and made road and street improvements.
8. Tear down sub-standard structures in the city while working closely with the public works department to enforce city codes.
9. When flooding occurred, this Mayor was waist-deep in water working side by side with public works employees to improve the drainage.
10. Spend 1.7 million to add and repair water, gas and sewer lines.
11. The Mayor and his wife worked the phones both day and night during hurricane threats.
12. He has served as president of the Chamber of Commerce, the Brazoria County- City Association and has been elected Man-of-the-Year in 1996 as well as Lion-of-the- Year in 1998.

With all these accomplishments, he garnered a 90% approval rating. Things looked great for this popular mayor.

Mayor Corley did not want to sit on his laurels. He wanted to transform Brazoria into an exemplary community for the rest of the nation. When he thinks big, he thinks BIG. So what can a leader of a community do to bring a better lifestyle? A show on Oprah Winfrey caught his eye. She

118

interviewed two young football buddies who happened to be of different races. One was white and the other black. The white boy referred to his buddy with the N-word while on the show, and Oprah stopped the conversation and asked the black boy how he felt about that word. Tears welled up and the boy admitted that it really didn't feel good even though this N-word had been a part of their relationship since infancy! The white boy never knew and upon seeing his friend's reaction also started to cry.

The Mayor heard Oprah ask the public to please stop using this word. Then the Mayor heard other black leaders like Rev. Jesse Jackson and Rev. Al Sharpton ask for the same thing. So he thought, "Let's ban the use of the N-word in Brazoria." That's what he sought to do. He asked for legal advice to see if it was possible to write such an ordinance for his city. After some study, and after discussing his plan with some leaders in Brazoria, he suggested the city council approve an ordinance to ban the use of this word and possibly fine those who used the word $500.00.

All hell broke loose. "How dare the Mayor infringe on our rights?" people said. "How dare he not let us use our term of endearment?" said the black community. The national media descended on this city in early February, 2007, and showed scenes of the town hall meeting the Mayor agreed to have with the public. Person after person wondered what had happened to their darling Mayor.

The Mayor's approval ratings have plummeted to as low as 10%. His reputation is so far down because of this one ordinance suggestion that the council will not vote on it, and the Mayor has been chastised to the point that he does not feel like running for election again!

QUESTIONS FOR DISCUSSION:

- What is the role of any elected official? Is it to represent the people or to be a leader? Why?

- What role should constituents play in this setting?

- Does the language we use play a part in civility in our public square?

- Who should decide what language is permissible?

- How should the use of appropriate language be encouraged? Enforced? How should the use of inappropriate language be discouraged?

Dahnke/Spath/Bowling

THE MEDIA AND CIVILITY IN THE PUBLIC SQUARE

When we speak to groups about the Institute, people often ask us about the role of the media in setting the tone for political discussions. We believe that the media along with the rest of us contribute to incivility in the public square, and the media can also choose to be part of the solution. The influence of the media, however, extends far beyond the dimensions of one individual's opinion or example, and therefore deserves special consideration.

So what part does the media play in all of this? Dictionary.com defines the media as: "**the means of communication, as radio and television, newspapers, and magazines that reach or influence people widely.**" This definition is a good start, but what about websites, bloggers, Internet games, music, movies and video games? All of these media are used to reach and influence people--often in deep and profound ways! There are many areas of life, including the media, in which basic civility is missing, or gross incivility is at play. But in a country that values freedom of expression, solutions are not easy to come by.

When we think of the media, we include all means of communication that reach a wide audience. We believe some media are used responsibly and well. Such use builds and strengthens the average human being and serves the public good. Other media is used less responsibly to appeal to the worst in all of us and to work against a sense of community or good will. The role of the Internet, movies and music in fostering violence, for example, is a topic of much debate.

There are news stories that inform the public about events that have occurred. Such stories can tell of a disaster like the tsunami that originated in the Indian Ocean in 2004 and caused such terrible tragedy. News stories about the tsunami affected all who heard or read them, and many people, agencies and governments responded to the news with donations of money, food and medical supplies to assist those affected by the tragedy. Such stories strengthen our human family by bringing us closer together to help people in need.

Then there are stories the media communicate that divide us. Politicians are often caught up in this. Our two-party-system pits one party against the other, and in order to differentiate between the two parties, the media publicize statements made by one side that contradict those of the other, often in provocative ways. We also see this every election cycle with the negative attack ads about which so many complain.

When we approach members of Congress to participate in one of the Institute's Congressional Student Forums, they often ask: "Will there be media present?" When we answer: "We can't make any promises, but we do not do press releases in advance of the event." there's often a sigh of relief. Why? The media often use soundbites that, intentionally or not, builds walls between individuals or groups of people. This is the kind of media that many do not appreciate. Yet it's the kind of media that sells! Sound-bites are quick, easy, and popular, and are an easy way for us to differentiate groups and individuals. Unfortunately, sound bites don't encourage us to give one another a full hearing, to ask questions, or to think through issues together. That is the hard work of building community.

CIVILITY: A PERSPECTIVE FROM INSIDE LOCAL NEWSPAPERS, BY MICHAEL ROBINSON (USED WITH PERMISSION)

I am writing from my experiences of working at two small local newspapers in Texas. A town's local newspaper is like a selective mirror of the town, reflecting the current news that can affect the lives of people living in and around the town it serves. Major news making bodies within a community are typically the city government, the school board, individual schools, local law enforcement, high school sports teams and church and civic groups. Ultimately, when one reads a community newspaper, one is reading about one's friends and neighbors.

At best, this selective mirror reflects the news with as little distortion as possible. But newspaper management, staff, and reporters are humans with personal opinions, agendas, and political motivations. One can only approach the ideal of objectivity in reporting and not reach it.

Because the local newspapers I have worked at are part of the community on which they report and the newspaper office is fairly accessible, citizens can and do criticize its newspaper in person, by phone, and in writing. Some write letters to the editor if they perceive that the newspaper has erred in its reporting or has not functioned in an objective or fair manner. These letters are published in the opinion section of the paper. On the business end, local business owners can choose not to advertise if they feel the newspaper is not serving the community's interest. By these means, readers have some power in holding the newspaper accountable.

As the saying goes, "One can't please everybody." There will always be some that will not be pleased with the stories that are published.

Some will be unhappy that certain stories were omitted or do not make the paper. The opinions expressed by local, guest, and syndicated columnists will sometimes make people angry. Ultimately, a newspaper is not in the popularity business; it is in the news-reporting business. Some news stories, by their very nature, can cast people, groups or organizations in an unfavorable light. An example of this might be a story exposing corrupt and dishonest practices by a local organization, official or powerful citizen in the community. Sometimes the newspaper plays the part of the messenger that can run the risk of being proverbially shot.

If the ownership and staff at the newspaper allow their political or social biases into the news they report in an effort to shape the government and social landscape for their own political ends, these actions can ultimately harm the trust that readers have placed in them and could have some negative effect on the tone of civility that exists within a community. However, if the newspaper sets its reporting and business standards high, this can set a positive example of fairness and respect that plays a positive role in terms of community civility.

Questions for Discussion:

- What role do you think the media play in setting the tone of discussion in the public square?

- Can you think of particular TV or radio programs that are uncivil in their format? Why do you think people do or don't watch or listen to them?

- Can you think of particular TV or radio programs that are civil? Why do you think people do or don't watch or listen to them?

- Are there particular forms of media that lend itself more to civility than another? Why or why not?

- Are you greatly influenced by media?

- Are the media influenced by the general public?

- How can we use the media to build greater civility in our nation, communities and homes?

END NOTES FOR RECLAIMING CIVILITY IN THE PUBLIC SQUARE: TEN RULES THAT WORK

1   Ismael Garcia, "Politics and Religion," Insights: The Faculty Journal of Austin Seminary, 120.1 (2004): 3-12, 8.

2   The Co-Founders of the Institute for Civility in Government have learned through their experiences that those who work as elected officials as well as their staff are hungry for civility themselves and greatly appreciate being treated as people, not pawns in a game.

3   Ismael Garcia, "Politics and Religion," Insights: The Faculty Journal of Austin Seminary, Fall 2004, Vol. 120, No. 1, 3-12, 11.

4   Recent examples include, "Heck, Blame It on the Press," rev. of Fat Man Fed Up: How American Politics Went Bad , Jack Germond, The Washington Post National Weekly Edition, July 19-25, 2004: 32; Gary Chapman, " Make way for the bloggers—they give us news with attitude," Austin American-Statesman, 23 July 2004: A13; David Broder, "Kerry's chance to rise above our divisions," Austin American-Statesman, 27 July 2004: A13; "Elevate discussion on nation's issues," Temple Daily Telegram, 29 July 2004: 4A; "The rudeness revolution," Austin American-Statesman, 29 July 29 2004: E1.

5   See the Preamble to the Constitution of the United States of America.

6   Donald K. McKim, Westminster Dictionary of Theological Terms, (Louisville, Kentucky: Westminster John Knox Press, 1996), 211.

7   According to Mary Jane Patterson, Director of the Washington, D.C. office of the Presbyterian Church, USA, "politics is love in action."

8   See Appendix 4 for a more detailed historical discussion of civility in Congress.

9   "George Washington's Rules of Civility: 110 Maxims Helped Shape and Guide America's First President," NPR, 11 May 2003, www.npr.org

10 "Our political ferocity is proving dangerous," Austin American-Statesman, 10 August 2004: A9.

11 See Appendix 5 for a more detailed discussion of participation in the public square over time.

12 David M. Wulff, Psychology of Religion: Classic and Contemporary, (New York: John Wiley & Sons, Inc., 1997) 162-164.

13 See Adele Faber and Elaine Mazlish, How to Talk So Kids Will Listen & Listen So Kids Will Talk, New York: Rawson, Wade Publishers, Inc., 1980, for practical tips on how to engage in effective dialogue on difficult issues, a classic and helpful guide for the parent-child relationship that provides useful tools for any kind of dialogue on difficult issues. See also Roger Fisher and William Ury, Getting to Yes: Negotiating Agreement Without Giving In, New York: Penguin Books, 1984.

14 David B. Guralink, ed., Webster's New World Dictionary, 2nd college ed. (New York: Simon and Schuster, 1982).

15 Buck Blankenship, "Listening Beneath," Meditations for Meetings: Thoughtful Meditations for Board Meetings and for Leaders, Edgar Stoesz, ed. (Intercourse, Pa.: Good Books, 1999) 12.

16 Peter J. Dyck, "Call to Unity," Meditations for Meetings: Thoughtful Meditations for Board Meetings and for Leaders, Edgar Stoesz, editor, Intercourse, Pa.: Good Books, 1999, 32, quoting from Dietrich Bonhoeffer.

17 Margaret Wheatley, Turning to One Another, (San Francisco: Berrett-Koehler Publishers, 2002).

18 See Stephen L. Carter, The Culture of Disbelief: How American Law and Politics Trivialize Religious Devotion, New York: Basic Books, a Division of Harper Collins Publishers, 1993, 230.

19 Richard C. Harwood, *Hope Unraveled: The People's Retreat and Our Way Back,* (Dayton, Ohio: Charles F. Kettering Foundation, 2005). Harwood describes people drawing back from the political arena.

20 "Few differences among the pews," Austin American-Statesman, 25 July 2004: A1.

21 "What's learned in political echo chambers? Nothing," Austin American-Statesman, 10 June 2004: Editorial page. Cass Sunstein, professor of political science and jurisprudence at the University of Chicago argues that when those who think alike discuss issues as a group, their opinions tend to gravitate towards the more strident positions as group members seem unable to envision objectively how they sound to others outside their group. See also George Will, "Study: Academia is liberal ... Duh!" Temple Daily Telegram,, 28 Nov. 2004: 4-A.

22 "Values do matter in American Politics," Austin American-Statesman, 12 July 2004: Editorial page.

23 "Values do matter in American Politics," Austin American-Statesman, 12 July 2004: Editorial page.

24 "Yes, Speech is Free, but Nobody can hear if We're all Screaming: Here's How to Talk Politics and Keep Your relationships," Austin American-Statesman, 12 October 2004: E 1.

25 "Values do matter in American Politics," <u>Austin American-Statesman,</u> 12 July 2004: Editorial page.

26 One example is a young friend of Tomás Spath's family, who graduated from West Point with honors. His early adult life is being shaped by our political system even as he serves his nation as an officer in the U. S. Army. Prior to attending West Point, he chose not to vote for many reasons. Among them are: the greed he sees in politics, the lack of caring for others in the system and the condemning that happens during each campaign. This is an intelligent individual who wishes our political system would change. If there were more civility in politics it would encourage him to fully participate with passion!

27 Henry Clark, "Community," 105-106; and "Society," 597-598; <u>Westminster Dictionary of Christian Ethics,</u> James F. Childress and John Macquarrie, eds. (Philadelphia: Westminster Press, 1986).

28 For example, Rep. Sheila Jackson-Lee, a liberal Democrat, and Rep. Tom DeLay, a conservative Republican, both supported a bill relating to adoption. Similarly, former Representatives Bill Archer and Lee Hamilton, a Democrat, frequently cancelled each other's votes. Yet they jointly introduced a resolution in Congress asking that the 1-minute speeches that Representatives are allowed to make at the beginning of each day be moved to the end of the day. Through the years these 1-minutes had become increasingly divisive and less civil. These Representatives suggested the House would be better served if the members did not start each day by blaming members of the other party for perceived inaction or wrong action during the previous day's work. The resolution did not pass.

29 House-Senate Historians, message board conversation with Richard Baker and Raymond Smock, October 1994, TM &, Scholastic Inc., 2004-1996, 94-10-07 16:14:10 EST.

30 "Presbyterians at the School of the Americas Vigil," Presbyterian Peacemaking Program, www.pcusa.org , August 12, 2004.

31 For a fascinating look at the effects of dishonesty on relationships, see Sissela Bok, <u>On Lying</u>: <u>Moral Choice in Public and Private Life,</u> New York: Pantheon Books, 1978.

32 Richard J. Mouw, "Religious Conviction and Public Civility," <u>Ethics, Religion and the Good Society: New Directions in a Pluralistic World,</u> Joseph Runzo, Editor, Louisville, Ky.: Westminster/John Knox Press, 1992, 98.

33 Richard J. Mouw, "Religious Conviction and Public Civility," <u>Ethics, Religion and the Good Society: New Directions in a Pluralistic World,</u> Joseph Runzo, Editor, Louisville, Ky.: Westminster/John Knox Press, 1992, 99.

34 Richard J. Mouw, "Religious Conviction and Public Civility," Ethics, Religion and the Good Society: New Directions in a Pluralistic World, Joseph Runzo, Editor, Louisville, Ky.: Westminster/John Knox Press, 1992, 100.

35 Richard J. Mouw, "Religious Conviction and Public Civility," Ethics, Religion and the Good Society: New Directions in a Pluralistic World, Joseph Runzo, Editor, Louisville, Ky.: Westminster/John Knox Press, 1992, 104.

36 Richard J. Mouw, "Religious Conviction and Public Civility," Ethics, Religion and the Good Society: New Directions in a Pluralistic World, Joseph Runzo, Editor, Louisville, Ky.: Westminster/John Knox Press, 1992, 105-106.

37 House-Senate Historians, message board conversation with Richard Baker and Raymond Smock, Oct. 1994, TM &, Scholastic Inc., 2004-1996, 94-10-07 10:14:10 EST. For a discussion of rules for judging when political debate is being carried out in a fair fashion, see a discussion by a professor of rhetoric at the University of Texas, Davida Charney, "Is a candidate playing fair? You can judge for yourself," Austin American-Statesman, 13 August 2004: A13.

38 House-Senate Historians, message board conversation with Richard Baker and Raymond Smock, Oct. 1994, TM &, Scholastic Inc., 2004-1996, 94-10-07 10:14:10 EST. For an example see Eric Uslaner, The Decline of Comity in Congress, University of Michigan Press, 1997.

39 House-Senate Historians, message board conversation with Richard Baker and Raymond Smock, Oct. 1994, TM &, Scholastic Inc., 2004-1996, 94-10-07 10:14:10 EST.

40 House-Senate Historians, message board conversation with Richard Baker and Raymond Smock, Oct. 1994, TM &, Scholastic Inc., 2004-1996, 94-10-09 22:33:43 EST.

41 Mark Juergensmeyer, Terror in the Mind of God: the Global Rise of Religious Violence, University of California Press, 2003.

42 Eugene L. Wolfe, "Deliberation, Democracy, and Dueling: Legislative Violence in the United States," pwolfe@ameritech.net, http://cas.uchicago. edu/workshops/cpolit/papers/wolfe.doc, May 18, 2004, 3

43 World Book Encyclopedia, Chicago: World Book-Childcraft International, Inc., 1979, Vol. 9, 30b-31.

44 Eugene L. Wolfe, "Deliberation, Democracy, and Dueling: Legislative Violence in the United States," pwolfe@ameritech.net, http://cas.uchicago. edu/workshops/cpolit/papers/wolfe.doc, May 18, 2004; World Book Encyclopedia, Chicago: World Book-Childcraft International, Inc., 1979, Vol. 16, 134a.

45 Eugene L. Wolfe, "Deliberation, Democracy, and Dueling: Legislative Violence in the United States," pwolfe@ameritech.net, http://cas.uchicago. edu/workshops/cpolit/papers/wolfe.doc, May 18, 2004.

46 House-Senate Historians, message board conversation with Richard Baker and Raymond Smock, October 1994, TM &, Scholastic Inc., 2004-1996, 94-10-05 15:48:32 EST.

47 Eugene L. Wolfe, "Deliberation, Democracy, and Dueling: Legislative Violence in the United States," pwolfe@ameritech.net, http://cas.uchicago. edu/workshops/cpolit/papers/wolfe.doc, May 18, 2004, 3.

48 See "Ky. Voters fearful as campaign gets deadly," Houston Chronicle, Saturday, May 25, 2002, 14A, for one such account. According to the article, two candidates for the office of sheriff were killed and a candidate for the office of county clerk was the target of gunfire. The sheriff suspended absentee voting by rowdy voters in one county. See also Charles Mantesian, "Local government all over America is suffering from an epidemic of incivility," The Politics, Governing, June 1997, 18-22.

49 Eugene L. Wolfe, "Deliberation, Democracy, and Dueling: Legislative Violence in the United States," pwolfe@ameritech.net, http://cas.uchicago. edu/workshops/cpolit/papers/wolfe.doc, May 18, 2004, 5. For a fascinating look at the evolution of our current political parties that sees their fractious history as beneficial, see David von Drehle, "Origin of the Species: Political parties have evolved far from the Jeffersonian model," The Washington Post National Weekly Edition, August 9-15, 2004, 6. See also Max Boot, "It's much more fun to throw political mud," Austin American-Statesman, August 23, 2004, Editorial page, arguing that our current political disputes are tame compared to our history and perhaps if the disputes were more like those of our past more voters would pay attention.

50 For a comparison of our political discourse with that of the United Kingdom, see an article reflecting on how scripted our political campaigns are compared to the occasionally raucous activities prevalent in British campaigns, Mary Fitzgerald, Belfast Telegraph, "Seeking spontaneity on the campaign trail," Austin American-Statesman, Tuesday, August 17, 2004, Editorial page, A9.

51 House-Senate Historians, message board conversation with Richard Baker and Raymond Smock, October 1994, TM &, Scholastic Inc., 2004-1996, 94-10-06 13:22:05 EST.

52 House-Senate Historians, message board conversation with Richard Baker and Raymond Smock, October 1994, TM &, Scholastic Inc., 2004-1996, 94-10-06 13:22:05 EST.

53 "The rudeness revolution," Austin American-Statesman, Thursday, July 29, 2004, Life & Arts, E1. Other altercations: Rep. Tom DeLay (R-

Texas) and Rep. David Obey (D-Wis.) in 1997; Rep. James Moran (D-Va.) and Rep. Randy "Duke" Cunningham (R-Calif.) in 1995; and Rep. Sam Gibbons (D-Fla) and Rep. Bill Thomas (R-Calif), also in 1995.

54 NOW with Bill Moyers, Politics & Economy, "Election 2004---America Votes Overview, PBS, 1.

55 NOW with Bill Moyers, Politics & Economy, "Election 2004---America Votes Overview, PBS, 1.

56 NOW with Bill Moyers, Politics & Economy, "Election 2004---America Votes Overview, PBS, 2.

57 David S. Broder, "Election Day, Nov. 2, actually the last day to cast vote," Austin American-Statesman, August 19, 2004, Editorial page, 4A.

58 NOW with Bill Moyers, Politics & Economy, "Election 2004---America Votes Overview, PBS, 3.

59 "*Special Edition,* The 2004 Presidential Election," http://www.census.gov/Press-Release/www/releases/archives/facts_for_features/001643.ht..., January 6, 2004."

60 "Election 2004: Activists fight apathy among young voters," Houston Chronicle, Sunday, March 14, 2004, 15A; "*Special Edition,* The 2004 Presidential Election," http://www.census.gov/Press-Release/www/releases/archives/facts_for_features/001643.ht..., January 6, 2004."

61 "Youths choose social activism over politics," Corpus Christi Caller-Times, Sunday, March 21, 1999, Section A, A15.

62 See Morris P. Fiorina, with Samuel J. Abrams and Jeremy C. Pope, Culture War? The Myth of a Polarized America, New York: Pearson/Longman, 2005, which argues that indeed our political interactions are dominated by those with more extreme views.

63 "Youths choose social activism over politics," Corpus Christi Caller-Times, Sunday, March 21, 1999, Section A, A20.

64 "Youths choose social activism over politics," Corpus Christi Caller-Times, Sunday, March 21, 1999, Section A, A21.

65 Andrew J. Glass, "Americans not showing civic duty at ballot box," Houston Chronicle, November 31, 2000.

66 David Broder, "Representative government on life-support in U.S.," Houston Chronicle, January 2, 2000.

67 Lee Mortimer, "There's a very simple reason for voter apathy," Outlook, Houston Chronicle, Monday, October 9, 2000, 25A.

68 Matthew A Crenson and Benjamin Ginsberg, "'We the people' no more: Citizens now customers," Houston Chronicle, November, 2002.

69 Robert D. Putnam, Bowling Alone: The Collapse and Revival of American Community. New York: Simon & Schuster, 2000.

70 Neal R. Pierce, "Many don't vote, but U.S. democracy well," Houston Chronicle, March 1, 1999.

71 "Vote Informed, "Houston Chronicle, Tuesday, November 2, 1999, Editorials, 20A. For some evidence that younger people may be reversing the trend to less social interaction described by Robert D. Putnam in Bowling Alone, see "Herd Mentality," Pamjela LeBlanc, Austin American-Statesman, Sunday, October 17, 2004, Life & Arts, K1, which discusses the revival of the Elks Lodge in Austin, Texas, where younger members are joining the World War II veterans in an intergenerational form of social interaction.

72 "America the furious," Austin American-Statesman, Sunday, August 8, 2004, Insight, E 1.

73 Michael Jinkins and Debra Bradshaw Jinkins, The Character of Leadership, San Francisco: Jossey-Bass Publishers, 1998, Preface, xiv.

74 "Wickett city elections cancelled," The MONAHANS NEWS:Weekly Newspaper for Ward County, April 16, 1997. City elections scheduled for Wickett, Texas, on May 3, 1997, were canceled after only one candidate filed for the three seats up for re-election on the Wickett City Council. The City Council met and adopted an ordinance canceling the election and declaring the candidate elected to the offices for which they had filed as candidates. This procedure was permitted under Section 2.051-.053 of the Texas Election Code, adopted in 1995.

75 Terry Tempest Williams, "Engagement, The conclusion of the author's triptych on the open space of democracy," Orion Online, July/August 2004, www.oriononline.org, 7.

76 Lee Hamilton, "Speak Up to Congress," Houston Chronicle, August 29, 1999.

THE AUTHORS

REV. CASSANDRA DAHNKE is the Pastor at Woodforest Presbyterian Church in Houston, Texas. She received a B.A. in Sociology from Texas Tech University and a Master of Divinity Degree from Austin Presbyterian Theological Seminary.

REV. TOMÁS SPATH is an interim pastor in the Presbyterian Church USA. He obtained a B.A. in Spanish from Gettysburg College, and a Master of Divinity from McCormick Theological Seminary.

BOTH REV. DAHNKE and REV. SPATH have mediation training. During their time working at New Covenant Presbytery in Houston, Texas, they led legislative conferences in Washington, D.C.

DONNA CURTIS BOWLING is a writer, teacher, speaker and occasional preacher. She obtained her B.A. in Psychology from the University of Oklahoma, her J.D. from the University of Oklahoma College of Law, and a Master of Arts in Theological Studies Degree concentrating in Ethics from Austin Presbyterian Theological Seminary. More recently, she has served as an adjunct professor at Tarlton State University and the University of Mary Hardin-Baylor.